YEOHLEE TENG

First published in Australia in 2003 by
Peleus Press
an imprint of The Images Publishing Group Pty Ltd
ACN 059 734 431
6 Bastow Place, Mulgrave, Victoria 3170
Telephone +613 9561 5544 Facsimile +613 9561 4860
email books@images.com.au
www.imagespublishinggroup.com

National Library of Australia Cataloguing-in-Publication Data

ISBN 1 86470 003 3.

1. Teng, Yeohlee. 2. Fashion designers – Biography.
3. Costume design. 4. Fashion. I. Major, John S.
II. Teng, Yeohlee.

746.92092

Designed by Patricia McKenna and Yeohlee Teng
Edited by John S Major and Yeohlee Teng
Coordinated by Eliza Hope

Film by Mission Productions Limited
Printed by Everbest Printing Co. Ltd. in Hong Kong/China

YEOHLEE:WORK

YEOHLEE:WORK

WITH ESSAYS BY

PAOLA ANTONELLI

ANDREW BOLTON

RICHARD FLOOD

HAROLD KODA

MARYLOU LUTHER

RICHARD MARTIN

SUSAN SIDLAUSKAS

VALERIE STEELE

YEOHLEE TENG

EDITED BY

JOHN S MAJOR

YEOHLEE TENG

DESIGNED BY

PATRICIA MᶜKENNA

YEOHLEE TENG

PELEUS PRESS

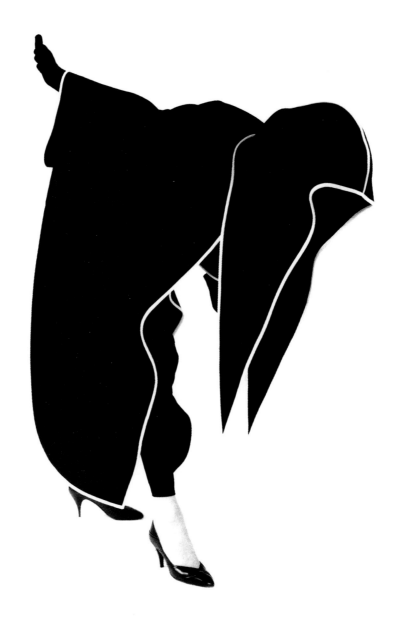

Fall 1982
Black wool melton hooded cape with
white wool doeskin piping

"Clothes have magi

Their geometry forms shapes that can lend a wearer power". – Yeohlee Teng

Contents

Yeohlee Teng Bryant Park 1997

PREFACE
YEOHLEE TENG

I approach fashion from a design standpoint, locating my vision within a cultural context. My purpose is to clothe, enhance, engage, empower and entertain. Fashion has to function, adhere to a standard in aesthetics, be fun and most of all succeed as clothing. Materials, seams and geometry make up the sum of the parts. Timing makes it fashion.

Clothes are animated by the body. How one sits, stands or walks and one's gestures are equally affected by design decisions. Where one places a pocket – whether it is a vertical, horizontal or diagonal slash – and its shape and depth, affects how the garment feels and the stance one takes. The shape and form of what you wear affects your movement, whether you sweep into a room or mince around.

Conservation of fabric, labor and time are part of my design decisions. It is important that my work does not perpetuate waste; that economy is factored into design. The width of the fabric and the design layout help to minimize waste. The seams that hold the clothes together are the decorative elements. One size fits all is a recurring theme. As a concept it is the ultimate in efficiency – from saving floor space to cutting time.

Clothing as shelter prevails within the body of my work, beginning with the pivotal exhibition "Intimate Architecture: Contemporary Clothing Design" at the Hayden Gallery, Massachusetts Institute of Technology in 1982. All clothes exhibited are now part of the permanent collection at the Costume Institute in the Metropolitan Museum of Art.

Clothes as second skin was explored in another exhibition "Energetics: Clothes and Enclosures" at Aedes East Gallery, Berlin and at the Netherlands Architecture Institute in Rotterdam in 1998. This installation parallels the discipline of fashion and architecture.

The notion of designing for the "urban nomad" came from my wanting to make clothes that one can wear directly to a meeting on a journey from New York to Kuala Lumpur. I like the clothes that I design to be versatile, multi-functional and efficient, breaking down artificial boundaries of what is appropriate to what is essential.

The clothes I design affect how people feel about themselves as well as how they are perceived. One can be enshrouded in mystery or encloaked with power. There is true magic in the ability of the clothes to influence not only the wearer but the viewer as well.

INTRODUCTION: LESS IS MOORISH

MARYLOU LUTHER

The first time I heard of Yeohlee was in 1982. The Milan designer Gianfranco Ferre had sent me the catalog from an exhibition on clothing design at the Massachusetts Institute of Technology's Hayden Gallery.

MIT and fashion? I was intrigued. Especially with the notion that clothes can be created from geometric forms deliberately distinguished from the organic curves of human anatomy.

Of the eight designers whose work was featured in the exhibition on "Intimate Architecture: Contemporary Clothing Design", Yeohlee was the only one whose work I didn't know.

Who was this "unknown" whose work was deemed worthy of sharing an exhibition not just with Ferre, who was trained as an architect, but with such other design legends as Giorgio Armani, Issey Miyake, Claude Montana, Mariuccia Mandelli of Krizia, Stephen Manniello and Ronaldus Shamask?

Who was this Malaysian-born New Yorker who designed the cover garment photographed by Robert Mapplethorpe? (See page 22.) The one described in the catalog as a coat, but a garment that looked very much like an academic robe to me. By the time I got half-way through the catalog to the Mapplethorpe photograph of Yeohlee's mysterious hooded cape (see page 25), shown in profile on a faceless model holding a crystal ball, I knew I had to meet her.

As it turns out, that khaki poplin cape, pattern on page 155, is central to Yeohlee's career ("it put me into business in 1981"), to her one-size design concept ("the ultimate efficiency"), to her principles of economy (the garment is made from one 3.25-yard length of 60-inch fabric with no waste) and constancy (it's been in every collection since that day in 1981 when Dawn Mello, then president of Bergdorf Goodman, put it in the store catalog). It is, she says, her favorite design, and the one of which she's most proud.

The simplicity of the cape is also an expression of Yeohlee's personal respect for simplicity in life. Like Robert Browning in his poem "Andrea Del Sarto", she believes that less is indeed more.

Sometimes, as in her "Less is Moorish" collection for Fall/Winter 2001, less became more inclusive, encompassing such ethnic inspired garments as burnooses.

Yeohlee sees this spare, artifice-free outlook as a reflection of her cultural heritage.

"In Chinese paintings there is often a landscape, then a tiny figure of a man," explains the designer. "To me, this relationship of man to his environment expresses a viewpoint of our relative importance to everything else – our role in the scale of the universe."

In today's ego-driven fashion ethos, wherein many designers see themselves as the center of the universe, Yeohlee's position is in exact keeping with her life philosophy. She's an important part of the fashion landscape, yet she has refused the concessions and compromises required of an enlarged role that might jeopardize her independence. She makes no obvious bids for attention. She has the ability to be still and quiet in the maelstrom of la mode. Yet she is a strong, powerful spokesperson for modernity, and an authority on functionalism in fashion. The fact that museum curators seek her work and architects her collaboration speaks volumes for her talent.

Yeohlee traces her minimalist leanings to her Asian heritage. She sees minimalism as a core value of Asian culture. I see her sensibility as being spare of add-on decoration, but not minimal in the sense of stark, reductive, rigorous clothes that are so strict, severe and purposely plain they're boring.

Yeohlee's clothes are subtle, not soporific. They are never trend-driven, yet they have driven trends. In the Fall collections for the year 2000, for example, European designers as well as American rediscovered intarsia – the use of inlaid patterns or shapes as a kind of surface decoration. Or, in the allusive apparel/architecture metaphor, bas relief. Yeohlee has long championed this way of modular fabric schemata as a way of transforming a fabric without embellishing it in the sense of adornment.

As Susan Sidlauskas wrote in the Hayden Gallery's "Intimate Architecture" catalog, "Her forms have a studied dignity that is almost ecclesiastical". I agree with the dignity part, but except for her capes and some of her more commodious coats, I don't see Yeohlee's clothes as clerical. To me, she is, indeed, an architect who just happens to be working in the medium of clothes, not buildings. Her clothes are wearable structures.

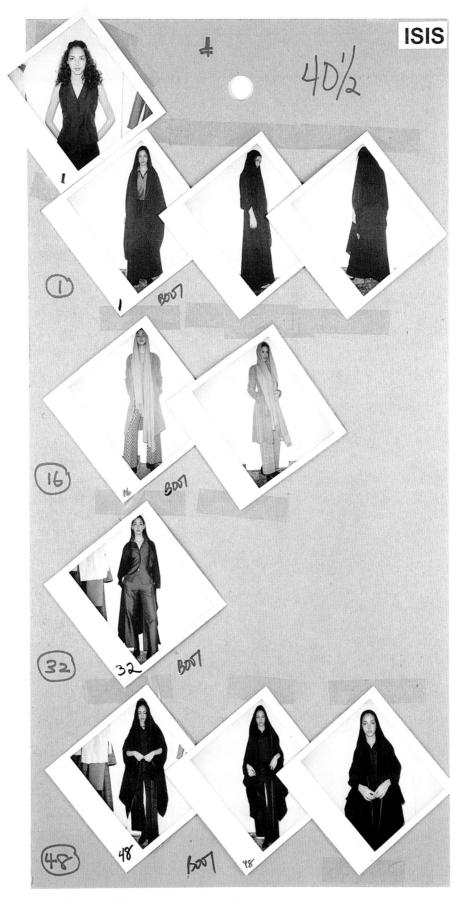

Dress card for model Isis Fall 2001 runway show Bryant Park February 2001

"Sometimes, as in her 'Less is Moorish' collection for Fall/Winter 2001, less became
more inclusive, encompassing such ethnic inspired garments as burnooses."

They not only provide shelter to the body, they seem to define the space around it.

Unlike Ferre, however, who often uses stiff, oblong collars and protruding bows to throw a dramatic shadow on the front of a jacket as an architect uses a pediment to cast a shadow over a facade, thereby creating a kind of impenetrable force-field around the wearer, Yeohlee does not set up such a distancing of wearer from viewer. Her clothes are strong, yet approachable. Her artful arrangements of geometric shapes and planes are user-friendly, and their aura is more a halo of empowerment than spatial isolation chamber.

To Yeohlee, empowerment is a by-product of good design. "If you put on something that makes you feel confident, it bolsters you, empowers you. The feeling can be very tangible, as in the case of the towering, empowering hats worn by Catholic cardinals, or very intangible, as in the sometimes mystical power of a color." "Somehow", she continues, "a lot of fabric has a lot of power, hence the imposing majesty of royal and ecclesiastical robes".

As one who wears Yeohlee's designs, I feel their power, and when I wear my black gabardine Yeohlee jacket with fly front I think of it as an investiture of authority. To use Yeohlee's empowerment simile, I know the jacket bestows me with a tangible fashion authority as well as an intangible feel-goodness that comes with the right fit and the right shape for my body. When I wear my classic black Yeohlee pants I thank God – and Yeohlee – that they've been treated to survive a downpour without ruination thanks to her use of stain and rain repellents. And when I wear my washable wool Yeohlee jacket, I'm grateful I can care for it myself and keep it free from drycleaning chemicals. As a consumer, I'm thankful that she's not one of those name designers who refuses to use synthetic fibers or techno finishes.

The late Richard Martin, costume curator at the Metropolitan Museum of Art until his death in 1999, described Yeohlee's clothes as "the synthesis of reason and magic". He was right.

The magic is, according to Yeohlee, in the magical properties of numbers. She says a jacket is made out of numbers at play, as in a 9-inch opening and a 9-inch armhole adding up to an unquantifiable measurement of comfort. And the how-else-can-you-explain-it mystical power of that first enchanting cape cut from a 3.25-yard length of 60-inch poplin.

I don't know if it's the supernatural, divine intervention, voodoo or her own passion for originality, but as if by magic Yeohlee has been able to avoid the retro virus that has plagued so many designers in the late 20th and early 21st centuries.

Her work is the perfect example of her definition of fashion as art. "Fashion", she contends, "is art with a function attached to it. It is an art form that only succeeds when it works as clothing. While art has emotional content, it doesn't have a real function. It may lift your spirit or reach your soul, but it doesn't keep you warm".

Yeohlee's clothes warm me, body and soul.

Fall 1998 Black gabardine fly front "Luther" jacket

"As one who wears Yeohlee's designs, I feel their power, and when I wear my black gabardine Yeohlee jacket with fly front I think of it as an investiture of authority. To use Yeohlee's empowerment simile, I know the jacket bestows me with a tangible fashion authority as well as an intangible feel-goodness that comes with the right fit and the right shape for my body."

Robert Mapplethorpe
Lisa Lyon, 1982
All Mapplethorpe works copyright © The Estate of Robert Mapplethorpe. Used with permission.

Yeohlee Fall 1982 White merino back-button coat piped in black
This image was used as a poster for the invitation to the exhibition and on the cover of the exhibition catalog

INTIMATE ARCHITECTURE: CONTEMPORARY CLOTHING DESIGN

SUSAN SIDLAUSKAS

Intimate Architecture : Contemporary Clothing Design
May 15–June 27, 1982
Susan Sidlauskas
Excerpted from the catalog and adapted by John S Major

Yeohlee Teng believes that the transposition of two cultures, her native Malaysia and her adopted United States, frees her to pursue a vision that is more idiosyncratic than the dictates of either culture. Her work derives from a persistent tug between the stasis of precise planes and the sweep of movement. Her forms have a studied dignity that is almost ecclesiastical. Poles of movement and stillness, light and dark, depth and surface are plotted out in meticulously articulated forms. A shimmering ripple in the line of a cape's hem finds echoes in the spiral seam of pants below.

Yeohlee locates her vision more compatibly in the art rather than the fashion world. Her geometric sheaths, on which squares or triangles float on a contrasting field of color, challenge spatial perceptions in a manner reminiscent of a Richard Serra drawing of a black plane skewed against a white page. Her capes are cowled robes with a jaunty swing that imparts levity to their imposing presence. She exploits contrasts in light and dark by dramatically positioning black lines against icy-white panels of a coat. Similarly, she challenges perception by making the spaces that ordinarily recede between pleats thrust forward in white.

Her spare vision lights on the essentials of form; while refusing to conform shapes to the contours of the anatomy, she always retains a concern for the wearer's comfort and mobility. Despite the fastidious, economical use of fabric and facility with drapery, both of which harken back to old couture, her juxtapositions and simplicity are modern.

Robert Mapplethorpe
Lisa Lyon, 1982
All Mapplethorpe works copyright © The Estate of Robert Mapplethorpe. Used with permission.

Yeohlee Fall 1981 Black wool doeskin "one size fits all" cape as it appears in the exhibition catalog
Pattern on page 155

"Intimate Architecture: Contemporary Clothing Design" Hayden Gallery, MIT, Cambridge Now part of the permanent collection of the Costume Institute, Metropolitan Museum of Art, New York
Details of each piece on page 27

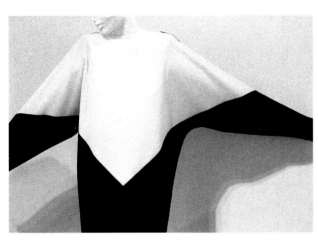

Fall 1982 Black and white wool doeskin dress

Fall 1982 Black and white wool doeskin suit

Fall 1982 White merino back button coat piped in black

Left: Fall 1982 Black wool melton hooded cape with white wool doeskin piping
Right: Fall 1982 Black and white wool doeskin fencing suit The jacket buttons at the back

Intimate Architecture:
Contemporary Clothing Design

KODAK SAFETY FILM 5063

KODAK SAFETY FILM 5063

Contact sheets of photographs taken by
Yeohlee Teng at MIT of the exhibition
"Intimate Architecture: Contemporary Clothing Design" 1982

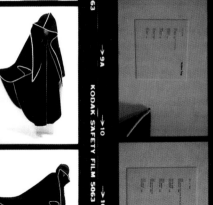

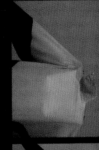

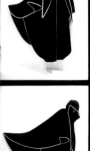

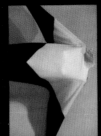
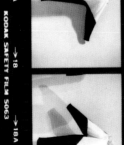

OF GOOD CLOTHES
AND GOOD DESIGN

PAOLA ANTONELLI

Good design may be described as a combination of lucid strategy, speculative interest in other human beings and aesthetic talent. It then follows that some particular instances of clothing design naturally belong to the field of design studies. And some instances have indeed been rescued away from the history of the decorative arts already. From such a straightforward point of view, design encompasses many more expressions than merely architecture, graphics and the making of objects. This categorical distinction among different forms of design is a consequence of our analytical approach to the world of creativity. Although in older times these distinctions did not seem necessary, the aftermath of the industrial revolution has fragmented visual culture into high and low in a new fashion no longer based only on quality, but also on production methods. Initially industrial was bad, crafted was good. Then the machine became the paradigm and all that was handmade was unenlightened. A few decades later, in the 1960s, what could not be shared with the mass market could not be right and earnest. In other words, we have spent decades dividing, juxtaposing and comparing. Yet, recently, designers like Yeohlee push us to bridge this gap once again and prepare our critical approach to post-industrial, universal design.

The criteria that can be applied to appreciate clothing design are indeed the same that apply to industrial design and even to architecture. The architect's job as a matter of fact consists of designing not only mere shelters, but also, and more importantly, symbolic spaces. How respectful and efficient they are in regard to these primary needs – and how much talent, personality and innovative energy they exercise in the process – is one measure of their resonance and ultimately of their success. The same can be said about designers who focus on objects instead of buildings and who have the same intangible responsibility. Designers' work, moreover, is directly based on dissemination and on their knowledge and understanding of other humans. It has to take into account economy of thought, function and materials, as well as beauty and formal affordability by a wide range of people, marketing and technological innovation. All differences between clothes, chairs and cars are resolved from the point of view of design.

QQQQ What is a mimbari? F98 #35 and #36. One size fits all.

Fall 1998 Look 36 Gray silk cape Gray silk tank dress See page 165

Fall 1998 Look 35 Gray silk mimbari "one size fits all" gown See page 165

QQQQ Where does that come from? The pockets? F99 #3

Fall 1999 Look 1 Black/navy laminated wool holster tie pocket coat
Navy laminated zip front vest

Detail holster tie pocket

Fall 1999 Look 3 Black silk dolman sleeve T Black laminated wool holster tie pocket skirt

Holster tie pocket skirt detail

babas

NOTE: Fall 1998. Apparently there is a strong influence of her Muslim origins, in that there is something very sensual about women being all covered up. Nyonas and Babas are the female and male counterparts of a culture that is melded from inter-marriage between ethnic Malays and overseas Chinese.

Spring 1994 Look 8 White handkerchief linen mandarin top Natural linen pedal pusher

Spring 1994 Look 10 White handkerchief linen short sleeve top Natural linen short

Spring 1994 Look 11 White handkerchief linen mandarin tunic Natural linen pant

Spring 1994 Look 33 Stone gray silk georgette "baju panjang" Stone gray silk georgette cowl top Stone gray silk georgette pant

nyonas

Spring 2001 Look 34 Cream cotton knit cardigan Cream cotton knit bikini top
Orange mélange tropical wool/linen tubular sarong

Spring 2001 Look 18 Khaki cotton pique zigzag kimono jacket White cotton interlock bandeau
White cotton interlock two piece back wrap sarong

Spring 2001 Look 57 Gold chantilly lace kebaya Merlot silk charmeuse tubular sarong

Fall 2001 Look 25 Tile sequin halter shirt Champagne silk satin slim pant
Champagne silk satin sarong laki laki

In the catalog to "Clothes and Enclosures", the unusual exhibition held at the Aedes East Gallery in Berlin in 1998, which paired Yeohlee's work with architectural models and drawings by T. R. Hamzah and Yeang, Yeohlee is hailed "the new Bernard Rudofsky". The late Rudofsky is a fundamental figure in the world of architecture and design of this century. A paladin of the commonsensical, extraordinary beauty that can be inspired by the observation of the world, he devoted himself to teaching curiosity and observation to his public as a means of elevating one's understanding of architecture and design, and ultimately one's life. He wrote, taught, organized exhibitions – full disclosure: he was a curator at the Museum of Modern Art, where this writer also works, in the 1950s and 1960s. He was omnivorous. He designed anything, from buildings to sandals – the famous Bernardo Sandals, inspired by ancient Rome, became all the fad of New York in the 1950s – and among his most important exhibitions are "Architecture Without Architects" 1964 and "Are Clothes Modern?" 1944–45. In the former, he showed black and white photographs of vernacular architecture from all over the world, from Yemen to Liguria, in order to highlight the dramatic modernity that comes from traditional culture. In the latter, he lashed out at the absurdities and constrictions characteristic of so much fashion of his time, in favor of the lasting beauty spawned by comfort.

The similarities with Yeohlee's work are immediately apparent, and not only because of the coupling of architecture and clothing design in the German exhibition. The truth is, Yeohlee is also restlessly curious and able to absorb inspirations from several different sources. In the Spring of 1997, her collection was inspired by the different religions of the world. In the Fall of the same year, it was all about living in New York. Her latest collections have featured many versions of sarongs – both a seed from her childhood and a very sensible way for many women of many sizes to be equally elegant. Yet, she has a special way of choosing and using textiles and of coupling the traditional skirt with contemporary tops and jackets in innovative materials. The technology she uses is both very new and very old. Like one of the most talented women designers of today, the Dutch Hella Jongerius, and like Rudofsky in his time, Yeohlee is able to take ideas from other cultures and times and translate them into Western manufacturing processes and languages of today. Her designs never mimic or imitate, but rather take the lesson and make it ours.

Spring 2001 Tubular "kain" sarong

QQQQ What is the difference between one of her patterns and an architectural blueprint?

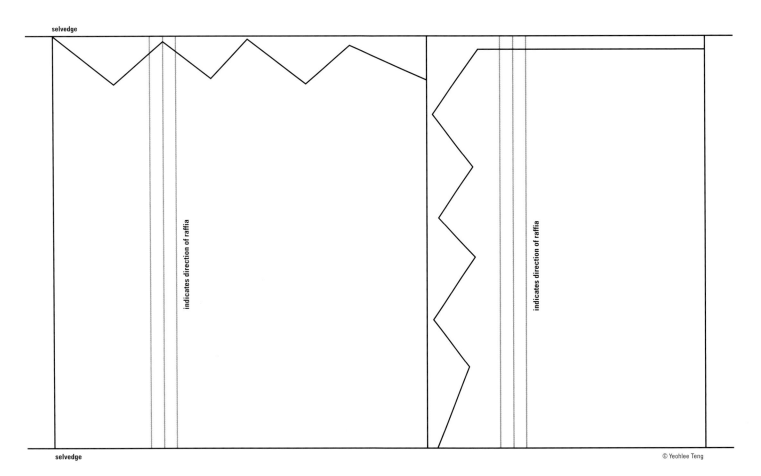

selvedge

indicates direction of raffia

indicates direction of raffia

selvedge

© Yeohlee Teng

Pattern for tubular "kain" sarong with zigzag seam pictured on right and page 41

KEY

——————— cut

– – – – – fold

Spring 2001 Look 1 Tan cotton tank
Linen raffia tubular "kain" sarong with zigzag seam

Another characteristic of the contemporary design world that Yeohlee shares is the ability to generate spaces through objects. A very small object can generate invisible yet powerful personal fields that others can enter only when invited, although they are not delimited by physical boundaries. I call this kind of space *Existenzmaximum*, a word inspired by the German rationalist idea of the Existenzminimum, or the smallest possible dwelling unit in which everything fits as if in a puzzle. In the 1920s, these architects, among them Walter Gropius and Mies van der Rohe, were intent on delineating the characteristics and specifications of the kitchen, dwelling, apartment building or neighborhood in which human beings could live efficiently while occupying the minimum amount of space possible. The Existenzmaximum is instead the shelter or device that, while occupying the minimum space possible, enables the human being to expand his or her vital functions. It begins as a small, yet comfortable space-enabling device where the physical boundaries are protective, rather than oppressive, thus letting the senses and the spirit roam free. Existenzmaximum can also be found in nature, for instance in a seashell, and then for instance in mirrors, in armchairs, in cars, as well as in many customizable minimal units of our times, such as the interface of a computer, a Walkman or a cell phone.

Yeohlee spontaneously embraces this idea with her clothes by designing a simple garment as a shelter that enables a better way to live and inhabit the surrounding space. The search not only for comfort, protection and privacy, but also for expansion and connection, is the engine that drives our choice of a space to inhabit. The concept of privacy has mutated to signify a private way to make contact with other human beings, with the rest of the world and with ourselves. The spaces that we find most comfortable are those that are designed to accommodate human expansion, and their functionalism lies in their capacity to initiate a chain reaction that transcends their physical boundaries. These spaces are usually designed to be used from the inside out, and the activity of their inhabitants is bound to put them under positive pressure. The exterior envelope is merely designed to contain and administer the explosion, and to expressively mediate the relationship with the outside world. Human beings are meant to impregnate them.

Spring 2001 Look 54 Black dewdrop beaded halter shirt Black silk charmeuse tubular sarong

Fall 2001 Look 42 Black matte jersey crewneck top Black silk jacquard bias sarong
See pattern and flat sarong pages 46, 47

QQQQ **Where do the design ideas come from? She admits to the sarong being a way to experiment with the fabric. She is doing the sarong to see how the fabric will behave. She will juxtapose biases.**

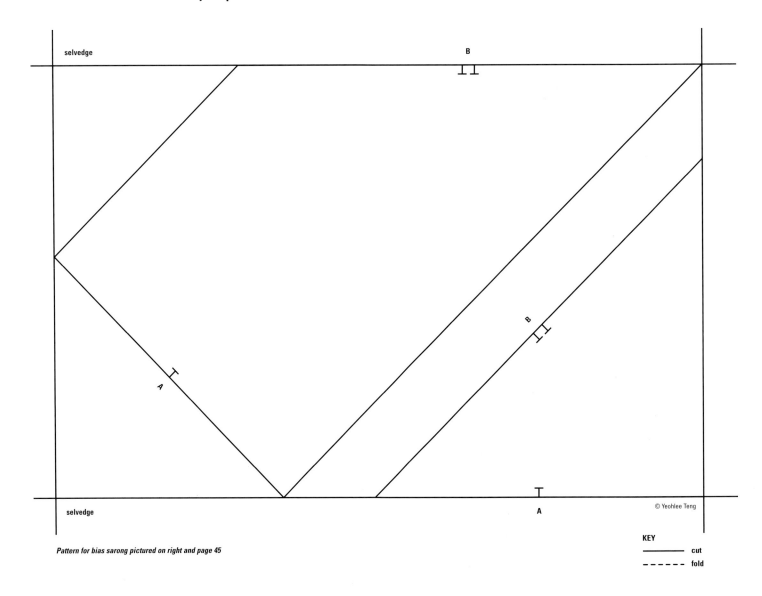

Pattern for bias sarong pictured on right and page 45

© Yeohlee Teng

KEY
——————— cut
– – – – – – fold

Fall 2001 Look 42 Black silk jacquard bias sarong See photo page 45, right and page 132

Fall 1997: Urban Nomads. Such a good idea, so appropriate for us, for NY, and for the times we live in. Clothing as a shelter. Traveling like yak herders. Wisdom of many centuries is transfigured into the clothes.

The affinity that Yeohlee displays with contemporary design methods shines through most brightly in her attitude toward materials and techniques. Even when she is employing highly sophisticated and removed industrial processes, she displays the self-assurance to be able to actually manufacture the objects herself. Firsthand knowledge of the technical possibilities of tools and materials is as important to a designer as the knowledge of anatomy drawing is to an abstract expressionist painter. It just shows, and it opens the door to creativity and innovation. A look at Yeohlee's older collections reveals in a more literal fashion just how deep her own skills are. Her evening wear of 1993 is as elaborate and sculptural as Roberto Capucci's. She knows how to build very complex shapes, which means she can graduate to building very complex simple ones. Because her design delight is so intellectual, Yeohlee does not have a constant style, but rather a constant interest in experimenting with shapes and materials. There is a range that goes from rigidly hypermodernist shapes to the coquettish Fall of 1995, where romantic and redundant accents are used in a stylized way, almost as a modernist interpretation. In the collection for the Fall of 1998, the shape of the clothes was dictated by the composition of the fabric, laid out in such a way as to maximize its use and reduce waste. The design process mediates between the purity of the idea and its necessity to live in the real world. That's what design is about: a pure idea brought to reality by using the compromises and the limitations of this world to make it even more interesting and beautiful.

Fall 1997 Look 44
Brown heather jersey coat with leather trim
Brown leather zip front jacket
Brown zebra pant

Fall 1997 Look 44 Back
Brown heather jersey coat with leather trim
Brown leather zip front jacket
Brown zebra pant

Fall 1997 Look 28
Midnight alpaca tweed coat with persian
lamb shawl collar
Silver metallic sheer silk tank dress with
plunging neckline

Fall 1997 Look 57
Gold sequin coat with golden sable trim
Gold charmeuse cowl tank
Bronze silk taffeta pant

Fall 1997 Look 1
Khaki embossed wool manchurian
candidate coat Gold metallic sheer silk shell

Fall 1997 Look 45
Brown zebra coat with mongolian lamb trim
Brown jersey long sleeve dress with plunging
neckline

Fall 1997 Look 20
Gray mongolian kimono coat
Narrow tweed stripe vest
Narrow tweed stripe pant

Fall 1997 Look 48
Silver/gold moiré notch collar jacket
Silver/gold moiré pant

Fall 1997 Look 52
Black/gold sequin mandarin top with side slits
Brown silk satin pant

Fall 1997 Look 10
Moss stripe manchurian candidate coat

Fall 1997 Look 27
Navy mongolian lamb chubby
Wide tweed stripe jean

Fall 1997 Look 13
Gold metallic coat with quilt lining
Black Yeohlee "resistance is futile" tee
Black quilted pant

QQQQ Fall 1995, #29-31: Can I touch the rubberized felt?

Fall 1995 Look 29 Navy rubberized felt mandarin coat Brown lycra/wool twill shirt

Fall 1995 Look 31 Navy rubberized felt welt collar coat Brown lycra/wool twill dress

QQQQ Fall 1995, #44-46: What is techno knit made of?

Fall 1995 Look 44 Black techno knit dress with white crossneck collar

Fall 1995 Look 45 Black techno knit off the shoulder dress

I have compiled a casual list of some of the materials that Yeohlee has used in the past eight years: **alpaca**, **linen oilcloth**, **lamé**, **raffia**, **silk satin**, **plastic**, **waterproofed cotton moiré**, **rubber**, **cashmere**, **nylon**, **rubberized felt**, **Mongolian lamb**, **sharkskin**, **laminated wool**, **DuPont Teflon®**, **flannel**, **gabardine**, **gold sequins**, **canvas**, **putty silk**, **paper poplin**, **engineered stripe knit**, **zibeline**, **tulle**, **shiny silk georgette**, and several other names prefixed by **"high performance"**. It is a wondrous list that is symptomatic of an exciting time for design. Our perspective on the material world has changed dramatically during the past 10 years and has visibly affected also fashion and popular culture. After the sensorial and material overdrive of the eighties, the jaded inhabitants of the western hemisphere seemed ready for a new obsession, this time with simplicity and purity. New technologies are being used to customize, extend and modify the physical properties of materials, and to invent new ones endowed with the power of change. New materials can be bent and transformed by engineers and by designers themselves to achieve the design goals that they have in mind.

Materials seem indeed to be the guiding light, rather than shapes. In Yeohlee's work they provide the synthesis for her diverse inspirations. As a matter of fact, contemporary design is an interesting composition of high and low technologies. Many advanced materials, especially the fibers and composites that are at the basis of the clothing industry, can be customized and adapted by the designers themselves. Some advanced materials, both in object and in clothing design, actually demand manual intervention because the industrial tooling to work them has yet to be invented. Such is the case in design, for instance, of carbon fibers applied to the manufacture of small aircrafts, often laid by hand on a wooden skeleton. Very high technology, in other words, can today coexist peacefully with very low technology. That is why technology offers designers a new exhilarating freedom and the possibility to customize the production to one's possibilities and culture. This evolution has brought many local cultures to the forefront in unexpected ways.

It so happens that some countries whose material tradition is based on craftsmanship and whose economy is based on necessity, like Brazil, are being looked at as new paradigms in architecture and design.

alpaca

Fall 1998 Look 33 Ombré alpaca jacket See page 131

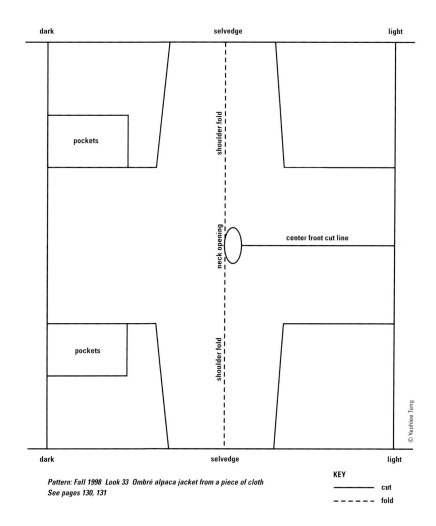

dark   selvedge   light

shoulder fold

pockets

neck opening   center front cut line

shoulder fold

pockets

dark   selvedge   light

© Yeohlee Teng

*Pattern: Fall 1998 Look 33 Ombré alpaca jacket from a piece of cloth
See pages 130, 131*

KEY

——————— cut

- - - - - fold

alpaca continued

Fall 1998 Look 28 Charcoal wool/alpaca horizontal stripe oversize turtleneck
Black flannel fly front skirt

Fall 1995 Look 26 Charcoal gray alpaca bathrobe coat with hood Black matte rubber jeans

Fall 2001 Look 10 Brown alpaca hooded cape Tan wool knit cowl Ivory flecked matte brown
double face pant

Fall 1994 Look 16 Brown ombré alpaca shawl collar coat

lamé

high performance

Fall 1994 Look 53 Charcoal lamé off the shoulder gown

*Spring 2000 Look 20 Stone high performance cotton zip front hooded coat Navy DuPont Teflon®
cotton elasticized waist pant*

Spring 1995 Look 61 Silver lamé sleeveless full length dress with high V-neck

silk satin

Fall 1994 Look 36 Brown silk satin high neck shaped jacket

Fall 1994 Look 49 Red silk satin shirred gown

Fall 1994 Look 45 Red silk satin jacket with tiger fur trim
Red silk satin pant

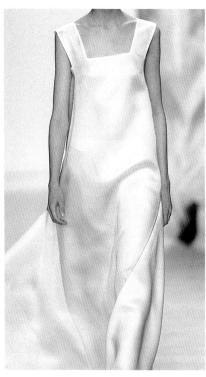

Spring 1999 Look 49 White silk satin square neck dress with
rectangular side flags

Spring 1996 Look 61 White organza halter crop top
White organza circular skirt

raffia

shiny silk georgette

Spring 2001 Look 11 White cotton grid eyelet halter shirt Linen raffia panel skirt

Spring 1998 Look 38 Black shiny silk georgette square neck tank dress

Spring 1995 Look 56 Cocoa raffia square neck ankle length dress

rubber

cotton moiré

*Fall 1995 Look 23 Black matte rubber and wool double coat Black matte jersey turtleneck
Black matte rubber skirt*

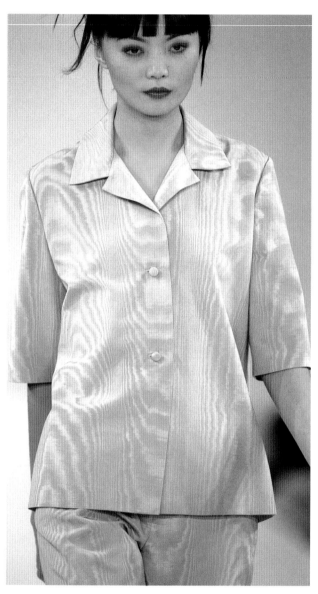

Spring 1995 Look 30 Sand cotton moiré camp shirt Sand cotton moiré jeans

*Fall 1996 Look 27 Black rubber coat with bonded velvet notch collar Black sheer shirt with
stretch satin sleeve Black velvet stripe pleated pant*

linen oilcloth

cashmere

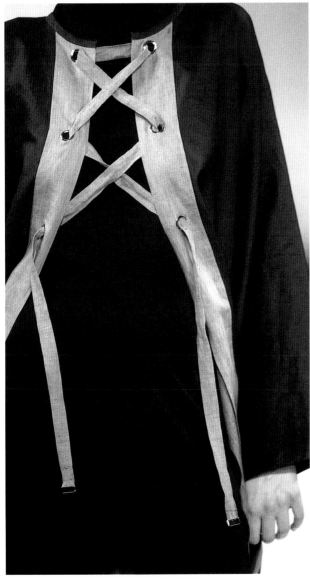

Fall 1995 Look 37 Brown cashmere boyscout coat Brown matte jersey crew neck top
Brown lycra/wool twill jeans

Spring 1995 Look 21 Black and blue linen oilcloth laced-front poncho Black matte jersey
sleeveless turtleneck T-shirt Black matte jersey leggings See page 209, right

Fall 2001 Look 11 Speckle moss cashmere/lambswool shawl coat with tie pockets
Heather knit cowl Matte brown double face harem pant

plastic

Spring 1995 Look 6 Iridescent blue plastic coat with attached scarf/hood White matte jersey cropped sleeveless turtleneck Navy silk/wool pique pants

Spring 1995 Look 46B Iridescent green plastic cocoon coat

Spring 1996 Look 14 Black plastic hooded coat

Fall 1996 Look 5 Clear plastic coat Black rib sleeveless turtleneck jumpsuit

nylon

Fall 1995 Look 22 Chocolate brown nylon trucker/cardigan jacket Black matte jersey crew neck top Chocolate brown nylon skirt

Spring 1996 Look 26 Banana bonded nylon mandarin jacket White matte jersey crew Banana bonded nylon short

Spring 1996 Look 43 Moonbeam stretch nylon satin sleeveless shirt Moonbeam stretch nylon satin circular skirt

Fall 1996 Look 1 Black nylon rib jumpsuit

mongolian Lamb

sharkskin

Fall 1997 Look 45 Brown zebra coat with mongolian lamb trim Brown jersey long sleeve dress with plunging neckline

Fall 1997 Look 31 Charcoal sharkskin racer back dress

Fall 1997 Look 43 White mongolian lamb chubby Brown zebra bias skirt

gabardine

DuPont Teflon®

Spring 1998 Look 40 Black gabardine trench

Spring 1999 Look 7 White DuPont Teflon® cotton displaced side seam dress / kangaroo pockets

Fall 2000 Look 13 Champagne lambswool "Heidi" coat Champagne lambswool pant

flannel

Fall 1994 Look 35 Gray flannel double breasted jacket with brown silk satin trim Brown silk satin pant

Fall 2001 Look 1 Gray silk flannel halter shirt Ivory flecked matte brown double face tent skirt

Fall 1994 Look 30 Gray flannel turtleneck dress

sequins

Spring 1998 Look 51 Avocado sequin bias drawstring dress

Fall 1998 Look 41 Sequin spaghetti strap top

Fall 1998 Look 46 Sequin drop waist "Klimt" dress

canvas

Spring 1998 Look 25 Black canvas bias zip front jacket Black canvas bias pants

Spring 1998 Look 31 Honey canvas crop shirt with zibeline trim Honey canvas capri

Spring 2000 Look 2 Teak cotton canvas L pocket vest Teak cotton canvas skirt with back fin

putty silk

tulle

Spring 2000 Look 50 Putty silk jacquard V-neck tank Putty silk jacquard sarong skirt

Spring 1998 Look 37 Gold sequin sleeveless top with tulle T-front Gold sequin capri

Spring 1999 Look 39 Smocked tulle sequin sweater

zibeline

Spring 1998 Look 35 White zibeline square neck tank top Gold sequin drawstring pant

Spring 2001 Look 41 White silk zibeline tulip jacket Orange mélange tropical wool/linen constructed sarong

Fall 1998 Look 10 Black silk zibeline notch collar shirt Khaki wool/alpaca wrap skirt with charcoal stripe on selvedge

engineered stripe knit

paper poplin

Spring 1998 Look 23 Engineered stripe knit shell Black canvas bias skirt

*Spring 2000 Look 19 Navy paper poplin zip front jacket with back vent
Limestone gabardine pant*

*Spring 2000 Look 26 White bubble back zip tank Navy paper poplin skirt with two
oblique triangles*

QQQQ What are the characteristics of Teflon? F99 #30-33.
Spill (?) and stain resistance only? How does the body breathe?

Fall 1999 Look 30 White knit DuPont Teflon® man's coat White knit DuPont Teflon® vest

Fall 1999 Look 31 White knit DuPont Teflon® hunting jacket Black wool/lycra skirt

Fall 1999 Look 33 White knit DuPont Teflon® high V-neck coat

I have a refrain I use to express how good and interesting contemporary design is, how it has no typological or stylistic boundaries, and how it is based on the real substance of science and art. It goes like this: the best objects of today are those whose presence expresses history and contemporaneity; those which exude humors of the material culture that generated them, while at the same time speak a global language; those which carry a memory and an intelligence of the future; those which are like great movies in that they either spark a sense of belonging – in the world, in these exciting times of cultural and technical possibilities – while also managing to carry us to places we have never visited. The best contemporary objects are those which express consciousness by displaying the reasons why they were made and the process that led to their making. It indeed also applies to Yeohlee's work.

NOTE: the preceding notes were jotted down by the writer in the course of her conversations with the designer and while studying the collection books. Spring/Summer 2000

FASHIONING THOUGHTS

HAROLD KODA

Harold Koda and Yeohlee Teng
at the Costume Institute,
the Metropolitan Museum of Art,
March 26, 2001

YEOHLEE > *Lots of people have interviewed me about my work, and I've talked a good deal about what I think my work is about. This time, rather than a question and answer/interview format, I thought that we would both talk and at the same time look at the pictures I brought of my work.*

Since you have some of my clothes in the collection of the Metropolitan Museum's Costume Institute, I thought we might start by talking about them. Now I am trying to remember, but I think these three pieces were the first pieces that you acquired for the Met. What interested you about them?

HK > Well, my interest in you started because of the show at MIT. You were always on my radar because your work has approached costume-related problems in ways that I like; for example, your foregrounding of the technical resolution associated with the engagement of a structure on the body, sometimes acknowledging the body, sometimes pulling away from the body. It seemed to me, especially in your early work, that you were actually orchestrating a denial of the body. So I was already in a sense prepared when you first called me, because those were my preconceptions at the time. I don't know if you remember this, but you said, "You haven't come to the collection. Why don't you come down and see it?" I think you felt that some especially interesting things were happening; that the most recent direction of your design investigation was exciting to you.

I actually had no other knowledge of your work except for reports by Anne Marie Schiro in the *New York Times.* When she would describe a remarkable raincoat, it seemed like some interesting construction was going on. She invariably focused on a Yeohlee coat. You know, she would always give a fuller description of one or two pieces in your collection. I would read about them, but usually the *Times* would print photos of something other than the pieces that were being reported! So I was approaching it basically as a naïf when I came to your studio. When I arrived, you came out and said, "Since you weren't able to come to the show itself, why don't you look at it on the video". You had placed a number of pieces against the wall from the collection, I mean all the pieces that you thought were the most important. I watched the video and surprisingly it seemed to substantiate all the things that I had imagined reading the *Times.* My expectations were actually fulfilled on seeing the video and the things on the wall.

I actually had no other knowledge of your work except for reports by Anne Marie Schiro in the New York Times. *When she would describe a remarkable raincoat, it seemed like some interesting construction was going on. She invariably focused on a Yeohlee coat.*

Fall 1996 Look 8 Black nylon stand-up collar "Stalin" coat with black quilt liner

Fall 1996 Look 8 "Stalin" coat worn open showing matching nylon quilt jumpsuit

I would say this particular donation, or this group of acquisitions, for us was similar to what we've just done with Geoffrey Beene. In both these instances, the designer has a sense that particular works are somehow beyond other efforts. There is an acknowledgment during the creative process that the work is outside the generally operating mechanisms of their larger body of work: which is, you know, inflected by commerce; design, but commerce also. These works are special because they break some boundary for the designer. The reason I mention Mr Beene is that he has just donated 200 things to us. But the selection was made from his archive, so the designer himself had already established some sense of the work's distinction.

In effect, we selected from his selection, which is relatively rare. And I do think it requires me, the curator, to think about the work in a slightly different way. Another dimension is added. It is an instance when the assessment of the design is not purely a curatorial construction. It mutes a little, perhaps only a very little, the subjectivity of the curator. So I think when I was selecting from this collection, part of the reason it was easy was because I was choosing from a pre-edited group — something more concentrated and reduced. What I try to represent in the museum, beyond examples of a period or of some expression of creative ingenuity and advance, are the distinctive qualities of individual artists, their signatures. And this particular collection was really a fulfillment of that.

It was a rather peculiar way of bringing things into the collection. I mean peculiar in the sense of atypical. It doesn't normally happen this way. Usually the work is edited through the process of the market, being purchased by a client, which automatically suggests there is the possibility of the object's transformation away from the ideal of the designer, you know, the size, the height, sometimes even the fabric. But in this case it was purely the designer and the museum, an acknowledgment together that this work warranted preservation.

YEOHLEE > *That's pretty interesting. You know, I don't remember most of that.*

HK > It was the first time I really got to talk to you. I think we had met before, because when I got your call I know I had some sense of familiarity with you but I don't remember what the circumstance was, whether it was an opening or something. But I know it wasn't a scary thing, where I was going to a designer who I had no face for, whose work I might not find sympathetic. On the other hand, I hadn't gone to any of your shows. My only prior knowledge was Anne Marie's reviews and the MIT catalog and some photographs that Ron Shamask had taken of the MIT installation. So now after that long preface, I can describe how I responded to your work on that first visit.

Immediately what struck me as I viewed this collection was the restricted palette; the use of an extraordinary textile which I don't think was that easy to manipulate; the sense of different planes playing over the topography of the body.

Immediately what struck me as I viewed this collection was the restricted palette; the use of an extraordinary textile which I don't think was that easy to manipulate; the sense of different planes playing over the topography of the body. There are some examples where you use softer fabrics that actually play off the body, but in this collection you didn't really express the body so much. These pieces, even off the body, had an inherent structure.

On the other hand, the pattern pieces did acknowledge the body. When you looked at the clothes on the models in the video you realized the body – that three-dimensional shape – became subject to an unexpected expression of planar tectonics: where flat geometries appear somehow to become more supple, and engage the body. I thought it was very interesting.

I'm embarrassed to say that it took me another eight years, no, nine years, to find out that what I was reading as pattern pieces was in fact the fabric itself (shown right). If I had known that then, it would have made the work even more interesting to me. You had played with the displacement of the textile's inherent border, I mean, its integral border. You were revealing the shifts, the misalignments, as a decorative element, but in doing so, you were disclosing the process of constructing this carapace.

Ivory double face silk satin jacquard with black border
See fabric pages 78, 79, 82, 83, 102, 103, 104

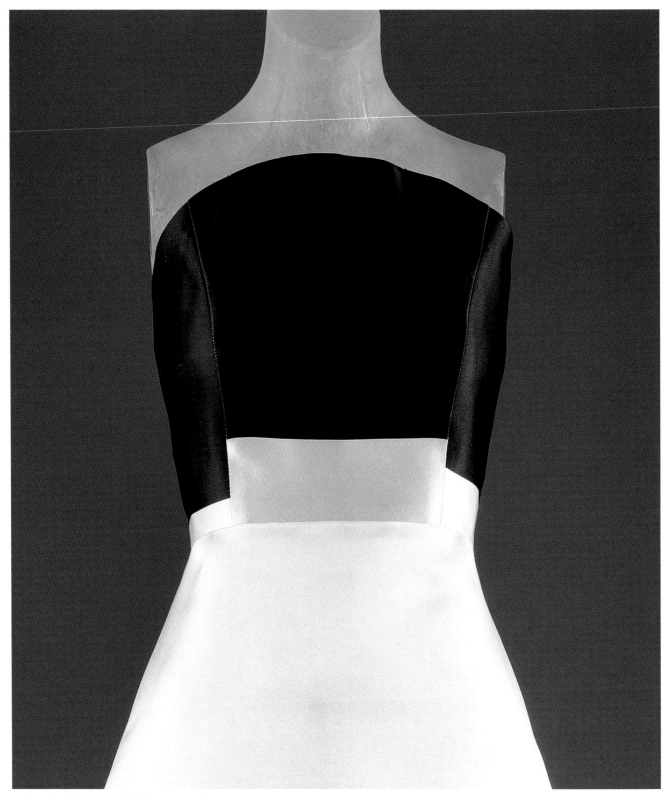

The Metropolitan Museum of Art, gift of Yeohlee Teng, 1995 (1995, 72.1)

... you insert elements that test the conventions, or make clear that you are not conforming to precedent. There is no reason that the alignments couldn't have been black straight across. By shoving it up you're saying, in effect, this is integral to the textile, and I want to reveal it.

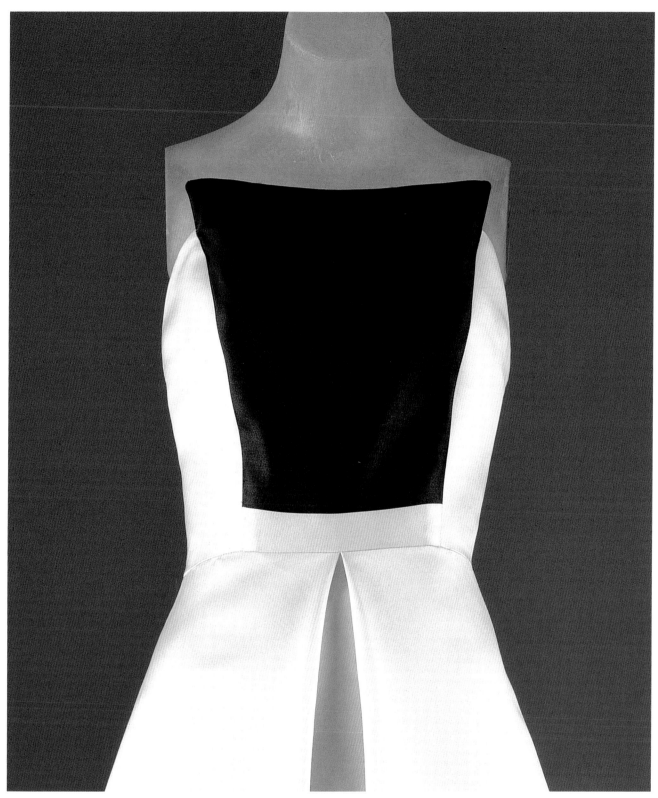

The Metropolitan Museum of Art, gift of Yeohlee Teng, 1995 (1995, 72.2)

... in terms of developing the front, it's so Yeohlee. I mean the notion of a plastron, the inversion of things, and playing with the edge, are familiar Yeohlee-isms.

Fall 2001 Look 13 Speckle moss cashmere/lambswool kimono coat Gold three-quarter sleeve shirt Khaki wool mosaic tie front sarong with herringbone waistband

In your last show, the look is very different, but there's still the same quality of two-dimensionality. You are constructing a system with your work, which has a focus, mathematical precision and order.

I love the way that, in this last collection, things pulled up and then wrapped around the waist. It was faintly weird.

It also suggests something, which in our conversations over all these years, I've always noticed: your faintly perverse humor and perspective. While these dresses could be seen as very, very classical, a closer look suggests something else. A sort of "épater la bourgeoisie" skewing of conventions is discernable in the deliberate selection of a fabric in which the displacements could be acknowledged and become integral to the design. That's what your shifting of that fabric 1-inch up suggests, and yet all the grain is acknowledged, so it's not as if you are defying the integrity of the cloth. It is only with the textile's border pattern that you are able to express your desire to subvert conventional approaches.

YEOHLEE > *Beyond what you were talking about, that was the first time that I had indulged myself in a really expensive, couture-type fabric, and it was an imperative because of the cost to get these three dresses out of the 7 meters that I had budgeted for. So, you know, my interest in the three pieces contained that practical aspect as well as all the others that you've spoken about.*

HK > Again I think that experimentation and testing are what's interesting in terms of process. It is probably not the couture fabric that held particular importance for you, but rather the fact of your surprising response to the fabric that made you actually pick up the phone and call me. On the other hand, I think what's interesting about this group is it doesn't seem as though they

... you are inserting a third requirement of your designs, which is for the cloth to express its original identity.

So whether you drape, whether you tailor, there seems to be this desire to have the material speak about itself in a different or more apparent way than other designers.

This approach is especially visible when you let the selvedge remain.

are the result of a tentative investigation. For example, in terms of developing the front, it's so Yeohlee. I mean the notion of a plastron, the inversion of things, and playing with the edge, are familiar Yeohlee-isms.

YEOHLEE > *It's a recurring thing.*

HK > Therefore it isn't as if the designs are something that seem hesitant or immature. Though for you, it was a first experience, so you valued it in a different way than perhaps other collections which were more seamlessly evolved. But by looking at your work as a whole, it really is a continuous thing. It is not as if there was suddenly this break where the fabric precipitates a change in you. It doesn't. I think what's very clear is that there are certain preoccupations that you have that continue.

You love, it seems to me, the idea of draping, but with the approach of flat patternmaking. The idea of something pliable and soft and something that is two dimensional always seem to collide in your work. How those almost antithetical aspects are resolved seems to me to be a basic Yeohlee preoccupation. Textiles are inherently planar ... how do you deal with that? Your work always seems to be a tension between revealing the two dimensional and overcoming it.

Fall 2001 Look 22 Red wool check three-quarter shaped coat Pale gold silk georgette crepon tank Red pinstripe tie front sarong

The Metropolitan Museum of Art, gift of Yeohlee Teng, 1995 (1995, 72.3) (1996, 72.1) (1995, 72.2)

... that was the first time that I had indulged myself in a really expensive, couture-type fabric, and it was an imperative because of the cost to get these three dresses out of the 7 meters that I had budgeted for. So, you know, my interest in the three pieces contained that practical aspect as well as all the others that you've spoken about. – YT

A sort of "épater la bourgeoisie" skewing of conventions is discernable in the deliberate selection of a fabric – see page 77 – in which the displacements could be acknowledged and become integral to the design. That's what your shifting of that fabric 1-inch up suggests, and yet all the grain is acknowledged so it's not as if you are defying the integrity of the cloth. It is only with the textile's border pattern that you are able to express your desire to subvert conventional approaches.

You had played with the displacement of the textile's inherent border.

... it's interesting that in two of the pieces you then do use it as a border, and you also use elements of it in the bustier. One is a plastron, one is the underbodice. But then again, you are introducing asymmetry; you are destabilizing something. – HK

From left to right:

Spring 1992 "Byron" Black and ivory double faced silk satin evening gown with sculpted bodice and back slit

Spring 1992 "Shelley" Black and ivory double faced silk satin evening gown with high waistline, curved bodice and A line skirt

Spring 1992 "Keats" Black and ivory double faced silk satin evening gown with sculpted keystone bodice and deep inverted center front pleat

Anyone working with fabrics, it might be argued, is doing the same thing. Where your work differs, however, is in the need to disclose the elements of design that are inherently invasive, even destructive, of the material. You like to show your interventions, or your violations of the rectilinear sanctity of the cloth. Most designers don't care.

In your last show, the look is very different, but there's still the same quality of two-dimensionality. If you think about ways in which you constructed the pieces in that show, you revealed the fundamental characteristics of the medium despite the very different quality of the fabric's "hang". The fabrics were so soft and fluid, but their essential structure, planar and rectilinear, could still be perceived. I mean, you could imagine unpicking the garments and then ending with pattern pieces reverting to their initial state, looking like simple yardage.

YEOHLEE > *I understand what you're saying, but it is a hard thing to talk about, because it sounds very abstract*

HK > It sounds abstract, but it's not. It's very clear and you do it. But designers know the difference between the tailoring and the dressmaking tradition, right? Dressmaking is often characterized by more fluid fabrics. The designer takes a length of it, goes around the dummy and drapes it, and pins it into shape, cutting away excess. Sometimes the pattern pieces derived in that way look really weird; they don't conform to the conventions of tailoring, certainly.

Tailoring is a whole other thing. The designer might still drape, or use slopers, generic pattern pieces. In any case, with tailoring the designer conforms more closely to established stylelines and traditionally shaped pattern pieces. The shapes derived from this process are generally recognizable to anyone who knows how to approach design in this way. But you are inserting a third requirement of your designs, which is for the cloth to express its original identity. So whether you drape, whether you tailor, there seems to be this desire to have the material speak about itself in a different or more apparent way than other designers. I don't know how else to say it.

YEOHLEE > *But that's very clever of you because I never really quite thought of these two aspects in the pattern manner. But if I were to go through books with you of flat patterns, you and I could say "draped"," pattern making", "draped", "pattern making". So to me that's brilliant insight. What you've just said is just so interesting to me. I never thought about that, but it's so true!*

HK > Most designers tend to have a bias for one or the other. And then the couturiers, you know, they just break the two ateliers apart. St. Laurent up until the early '70s said he could never do the flou.

YEOHLEE > *What's the flou?*

HK > The dressmaking, the soft dressmaking. It isn't as if the dressmaker can't make a jacket, or the tailor can't make a wrap skirt. But the mode of approach is so different and there is in both another aspect: the idealization of the pattern piece when it is undone. There are corrections and an idealization of the pattern pieces results.

YEOHLEE > *I don't like that process.*

HK > Well you don't admit it very much into your work.

YEOHLEE > *No, I mean the correction.*

HK > Right. That doesn't seem to happen. So what you do is you design things that don't require the correction. This approach is especially visible when you let the selvedge remain.

YEOHLEE > *Yes.*

HK > That seems to be one of your ways of resolving the issue of corrections. You seem to feel that if a technical design solution cannot appear aesthetic being what it is, simply expressing itself, then you don't do it. Or you would do it with hesitancy.

YEOHLEE > *But I also meant, you know, the strict patternmaking principle. You know, if you find a traditional patternmaker, trained in Europe or in that tradition, you will find that they will want to conform to strict patternmaking principles. And I don't like that. My work is more organic.*

HK > Right, but again it's the investigation and discovery that you prize, so the whole process for you will only hold your

interest as long as you're trying to devise something new. If it's simply a juggling of pre-existent forms and techniques, the most rudimentary kind of synthesis, that wouldn't interest you.

And I think that's why you insert elements that test the conventions, or make clear that you are not conforming to precedent. There is no reason why the alignment couldn't have been black straight across. By shoving it up you're saying, in effect, this is integral to the textile, and I want to reveal it.

YEOHLEE > *Well, we could take this further. With these two it is not on the same level. Right? Part of it has to do with conservation of fabric, I'm sure. But when you are dealing with fabric with a border, ending up with the black at the bottom is the most obvious solution.*

HK > But I also think it's interesting that in two of the pieces you then do use it as a border, and you also use elements of it in the bustier. One is a plastron, one is the underbodice. But then again, you are introducing asymmetry; you are destabilizing something. It's also what you gravitate toward when you're talking about things that interest you. Frequently the subjects or facts that interest you, at least in my recollection, are slightly idiosyncratic or even off-key. That you find fascinating! I think you like situations with an ostensible sense of normalcy with one element that's off-key or elements that are off-key. Still, no one would say your work wasn't very classical, since it has that cool conceptual quality.

The Metropolitan Museum of Art, gift of Yeohlee Teng, 1995 (1995, 72.5)
Fall 1992 Black double faced silk satin evening gown with ivory lightning band at bodice

I think you like situations with an ostensible sense of normalcy with one element that's off-key or elements that are off-key. Still, no one would say your work wasn't very classical, since it has that cool conceptual quality.

The Metropolitan Museum of Art, gift of Yeohlee Teng, 1995 (1995, 72.4)
Fall 1992 Black double faced silk satin evening cape with bells on points over ivory evening gown

... something like this is actually enhanced not when it is worn by someone who's fashionable, but by someone who has strength and power. Then it becomes sculptural, almost a performance piece or projection.

No matter how soft or drapey some of the fabrics are, you always retain a very strict line. You are constructing a system with your work, which has a focus, mathematical precision and order. But if it was only that, you'd be bored. So into that, you reveal to the viewer, or the wearer, some sense that, yes, while the garment is an aestheticized object, it is also novel thinking. You always insert something quirkish – I love the way that in this last collection things pulled up and then wrapped around the waist. It was faintly weird.

YEOHLEE > *But much of what you're saying has to do with your curatorial eye and your understanding of costume, fashion, construction, whatever. I think that a lot of people might not be able to read what you can.*

HK > No, my expertise is not necessary. You've explained that in this collection you were experimenting with extraordinary fabric. It was so luxurious. I'm just reminded that whenever I see fabric being milled, I can't imagine anybody would cut into it, even when it's greige goods. When you see the process of the making of fabric, you just can't imagine mutilating it. I imagine you must have had a similar sort of gravity of purpose to violate those pristine 7 meters.

YEOHLEE > *I did very well with those 7 meters.*

HK > I know. Your feeling of successfully exploiting the fabric was probably the reason for your calling me in the first place.

You know what else I see though, now, looking at it in retrospect? Maybe your frame of reference is much different from mine, but if I saw that on someone I would have thought: "Hmm, with all of that sophistication is this almost childlike gesture".

YEOHLEE > *What would it make you think?*

HK > Well, it reminds me of the French notion of the *belle laide*, the ugly woman who is really attractive. The thing that is so seductive about all those really kind of silly, feminine dresses, those girly dresses that Chanel did in the 1930s, was the women who wore them looked like Chanel or Mrs Vreeland. If you were young or pretty and you wore those models, you would have looked so inconsequential and trite. But if you had experience on your face, there was a toughness added to the prettiness that resulted in an almost paradoxical chic. So something like this is actually enhanced not when it is worn by someone who's fashionable, but by someone who has strength and power. Then it becomes sculptural, almost a performance piece or projection.

photo Deborah Turbeville

Fall 1992 Brown double faced silk satin evening gown on Ann Duong

Fall 1994 Sketches by Yeohlee

Fall 1994 Look 44 Black and white big check double faced silk satin evening cape

YEOHLEE > *You know, I love talking to you because I love to talk to people who open up little windows and doors and make me think about or consider things I hadn't thought before. It's very rare that that happens. One of the things that I treasured about my relationship with Richard Martin was that he would stimulate my mind that way. He would throw things back at me. For example, he said, "Your one size fits all is like an architect and a room. A room is one size fits all". And that would get me going for days, you know, I would be saying, "Oh my God" and "I love that!".*

So thank you very much. You are really helping me a lot. Actually, I'm at the point in my book where I'm really enjoying what I'm doing because I'm learning something from it.

I think that something that's never been discussed, at least not in any of the essays that were written for the book or any of the catalogs of my earlier work, is how instinctual my work is. It's totally instinctual.

HK > Because you're not thinking, "Oh, I'm going to do this because it's my signature".

YEOHLEE > *No, it's really an intellectual process. It's a thought process that gets realized in dimension. It is problem solving. Take this piece here, which you know was in the V & A's main entrance. This existed as a sketch just because it amused me to have this huge checkerboard. But now I've just realized here talking to you, that this season, Fall of 2001, I did red check pants. So there I go, I'm repeating myself without being aware of it.*

HK > But you know, what the check does is to reinforce the gridded structure of the weave. It is one of the earliest and most rudimentary forms of patterning textiles. If minimalists want textile with a pattern, they get plaids, stripes, checks.

Also, here's a fascinating thing that I've noticed. Frequently, if designers in the early stages of their career take an architectonic approach, they will deliberately go to stripes, not so much checks, but stripes. To me it's a way of reading the textile as you're manipulating it. To actually see what you're doing, a sort of subconscious reinforcement. For example, there is this extraordinary Balenciaga at FIT made from a thinly striped, ribbed fabric. He's made a spring dinner gown out of it. It's really about the way the applied or separate zones of the dress are in opposing patterns of grain, cross-grain against straight grain. The stripes are actually a way of reinforcing the architectural thinking of the designer.

YEOHLEE > *Now let's look for a minute at these. These are "Alice in Wonderland". They are some of my favorite pieces, in the sense that they are actually weirdly funny. This is the jester and that's the joker. They were actually called that. Here, this is the selvedge of that fabric, and to me it is the most interesting thing about this piece. And then if you can see the back of the coat from the inside, you'll see the selvedge of this fabric, and it isn't cut off. I just pressed it open. It looks quite interesting.*

Fall 1994 Look 42 "Jester"
Black double faced silk satin jacket with black and white big check collar
Black and white small check double faced silk satin bustier
Black and white big check double faced silk satin pant

Fall 1994 Look 44 "Joker"
Black and white big check double faced silk satin evening cape
Black double faced silk satin top
Black and white small check double faced silk satin pant

Which brings us to MIT. I think we should look at the MIT photos again and bring our conversation back around to that. This is kind of fun. I shouldn't be having such a good time. It's work. But actually, I realize that in order for me to get my book done, I have to really read and understand and digest and remember all the essays that were done about my work.

HK > But isn't your job more to think about what you were actually intending, and then finding where that coincides or deviates from everyone else's perception? Don't you enjoy it when you have actually pushed people to have larger readings, or maybe not necessarily larger, but different readings of your work than even you intended? That would seem interesting to me. I don't think you should just assimilate everything said about your designs, but you could say, "Oh yeah, that's interesting that they think that". Still, in the beginning, you should be clear about your personal intention, "This is what I think, and this is what the process is about". And you're going to find when you overlay that with what other people think, some of it will necessarily overlap. But the part that's really interesting is where your intention is being read in a completely different way than you expected.

YEOHLEE > *Yes, I think that you're right there. But in reading the essays I will say that Susan Sidlauskas had something definitive to say about my work, separate from what I was doing with it. You know, she had an opinion. Richard Flood had*

his own take on my work too. But his interest in my work was sparked by MIT.

HK > Everybody's interest was, including Andrew Bolton's. It's because that was such an important thing, that event.

YEOHLEE > *It was a very important event. I went back and asked Andrew how he learned about my work, and he said it was through "China Chic". Interestingly enough, my work has never been seen as especially Asian, you know, that Asian thing has never been brought forth.*

HK > I think why I hesitate about the Chinese thing is because if you look at some of your pieces, for instance the piece that was on the cover of the MIT catalog, one might think of China with the cloud borders, the sleeve structure, and the over robe. It seems so Manchu Dynasty. But really, it's not. Maybe it is in your unconscious, sort of percolating up, but filtered through a very fine-grained modernist sensibility. The conceptual part is not "the Dragon Empress", it is "a piece of cloth".
One size fits all.

Your things don't look like conventional Chinese dress, but there are aspects. So if I say a piece looks Korean, are you alerted to the possibility of something infusing your work, some manifestation of regional tradition? But even if it were, I think you have a slightly different approach. You don't mine the forms, instead you explore the processes. I mean you are closer to the designers who incorporate the strategies of regional dress, like the Japanese designers. Or the Belgians, who I think do it too. You are more taken with the elements of the actual construction of the garment rather than any explicit narrative. With the exception of your jesters, narrative plays a relatively small part in your work.

If you go to a show you can see, oh let's say somebody like Alexander McQueen, the savagery of the English against the Scots, a citing of history. You see it. It's a narrative. You go to Chanel and Lagerfeld conflates an 18th-century robe á la Polonaise with a Horst portrait of Chanel. With you, on the other hand, references are more elusive. Though I did have a sense with this last show that I was being presented an evocative theme, rather than an abstract concept. The show conveyed a narrative to me, but the individual costumes did not. Still, it's not as if I can say, "Oh, she's looking at Burma".

YEOHLEE > *I didn't do that. But what was the narrative that you constructed out of Fall 2001?*

HK > Well, I felt Bedouin, because it was like you were carrying your shelter with you. It struck me as a kind of nomadic theme.

YEOHLEE > *Well that's very interesting, because my Fall 1997 collection was dedicated to the "urban nomad". So whatever you saw is something that is one of my prevailing ideas, right?*

HK > What did you mean by "urban nomad"? Moving from city to city? Or moving within a city or ...

YEOHLEE > *Anybody who goes from point A to point B, you know, in the course of a day or a lifetime, is a nomadic creature. The whole thing started because I was looking outside my window and I saw all these people lugging all these packages, transporting themselves. And I was thinking also that I have a lot of friends who travel. You travel. You just came back from Bilbao. And then, I have friends who get on a plane and get out in Kuala Lumpur and go straight into a meeting. So these are the people I call the "urban nomads", because it's our lifestyle. So it's designing a very efficient wardrobe for them. That was the collection that had a lot of Lycra, DuPont Teflon® and easy-care machine washables. Again it was problem solving. The Berlin show that Richard wrote about started with Fall of 1997, which was the "urban nomad". Then the Fall of '98 was a furthering of the "urban nomad" idea, where we went into all the principles of one size fits all, utilizing the whole piece of cloth and so on.*

The Metropolitan Museum of Art, gift of Yeohlee Teng, 1997 (1997, 44.3) (1997, 44.1) (1997, 44.2)

From left to right:

Fall 1994 Look 43 "The Dormouse"
Black and white double faced silk satin small check
sleeveless dress with big check band across the chest

Fall 1994 Look 39 "Behind the Looking Glass"
Black and white double faced silk satin big check
high V-neck dress

Fall 1994 Look 40 "Alice"
Black and white double faced silk satin small check off the
shoulder dress with three-quarter sleeves

Polaroids of the lineup for the Fall 1994 fashion show

But coming back to Fall 2001. In November when I was in London, Valerie Steele and I had this on-stage "in conversation" event at the V & A. I showed a lot of slides and we discussed them, and I made some reference to my Muslim background. Then in the question and answer period, Andrew, who's sharp as a tack, immediately seized upon that as something nobody had ever discussed with me about my work, this Muslim aspect. So he wanted me to talk to him more about that.

HK > But what is that aspect?

YEOHLEE > *My answer to him was that I grew up in a Muslim country. So it's something that I grew up with that I'm aware of but that I've never examined, nor have I really consciously utilized it. Then he said, later on when we were having dinner, "It is so interesting that someone as articulate as you couldn't talk about your Muslim influences", and I said it is merely because I haven't really considered them.*

So in a way because of him, and because of Bradley Quinn, who was interviewing me for an article in Merge, *it was sort of like a challenge to me. So I decided that I would work on a collection that played on Muslim influences.*

HK > I didn't know that.

YEOHLEE > *Oh yes. They made me think about it and I said, "Hell, why not? Let's do it".*

HK > Oh, isn't that interesting! So this time it was a conscious decision.

YEOHLEE > *Yes, unlike a lot of my previous collections where I didn't do any research or make many references. This one I didn't do a lot of research, but what I did look at was Turkey. A lot of people didn't realize it was Turkey. I don't know what they thought.*

HK > Well, it, I don't think it looks like Turkey, but it does look ...

YEOHLEE > *Muslim?*

HK > Not so much Muslim ... or Muslim, but via the Iberian Peninsula. Like the way Spanish peasants lift their skirts and tuck the hems into their belts, that's what I saw. I saw those traditions. And because of your palette and the sense of the nomadic, I thought Bedouins. Although it actually has nothing to do with Morocco, or Fez or the Bedouin. So it's more an imprecise fantasy of what that other world is.

YEOHLEE > *But the soundtrack for that show was really important. You know, the physical environment of Seventh on 6th is extremely sterile, so the only opportunity that you have to create an environment is through sound and light. So the soundtrack was really, really important to me to generate a mood. And the person I was working with on the music, when he saw the clothes and the fabric, all he could see was tiles. Little tiles, mosaic tiles.*

HK > How interesting.

photo Alan Crespo

Spring 1995 Look 67 Black double faced silk satin evening gown with V-back and three-quarter sleeves on Gail Elliot

Fall 1993 Look 35 Ivory double faced silk satin lace front dress with half black sleeve (side view)

Fall 1993 Look 34 Ivory double faced silk satin lace front dress with half black sleeve

... if I say a piece looks Korean, are you alerted to the possibility of something infusing your work, some manifestation of regional tradition? But even if it were, I think you have a slightly different approach. You don't mine the forms, instead you explore the processes ... You are more taken with the elements of the actual construction of the garment rather than any explicit narrative.

Fall 1993 Look 31 Black and ivory double faced silk satin evening gown with black border center front

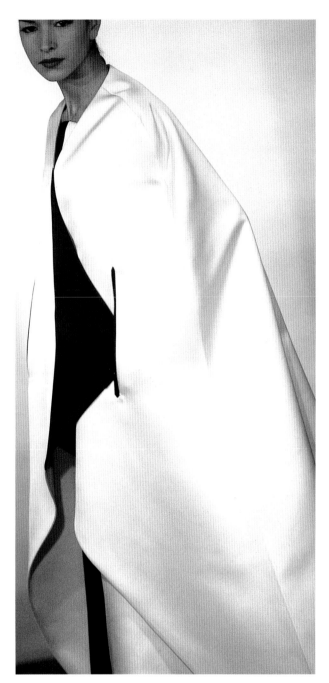

Fall 1993 Look 30 Black and ivory double faced silk satin evening cape with points made from black border

The Metropolitan Museum of Art, gift of Yeohlee Teng, 1995 (1995, 72.6) (1995, 72.7)
Fall 1993 Look 30/31 Black and ivory double faced silk satin evening cape with points made from black border Black and ivory double faced silk satin evening gown with black border center front

YEOHLEE > *I thought so too, because that opened another window for me. But, you know, beyond that there was another thing I was working on, because Muslim women are so covered up. I was thinking about how sensual and sexy can you be by being covered up? I was thinking, how much do you choose to reveal, and how much do you wish to conceal? So those were all the things that I was thinking about. And beyond that I was thinking about a piece of fabric. A piece of cloth, right? Some people focus on the Western tradition or the Eastern tradition. I'm not so interested in either as much as I am in the beginning of it all. In the beginning there was a loom and a piece of cloth. So whenever I do clothes, I like to funnel something back to that point.*

HK > But this goes back again to what I think about you, which is similar to descriptions of Mies van de Rohe. In the beginning, he was seen as the paradigmatic modernist. Over the years, however, his neo-classical allusions, his relationship to Schinkel began to be mentioned. But the modernists repudiated the past, right?

YEOHLEE > *Right?*

HK > And yet, history inevitably had its presence in their work. So now there are all these books and critiques of Mies that talk about traditional Japanese architecture, Chinese courtyards and ancient Greek rather than Roman classicism. And you can see it all in the work. But it was something that, as a modernist, he

wouldn't have acknowledged. He was probably not consciously referencing these things. It was so much a part of his unconscious, Jungian, maybe, or, you know, what Rilke called "blood memory". It was in his blood memory.

In the same way, I think of you purely as a contemporary designer, which is maybe why I'm saying that narratives don't percolate through your career. I don't believe that is what interests you most. Your primary intention is what you just described.

YEOHLEE > *It's ideas.*

HK > Yes, but it begins with fabric. I once knitted a sweater. I've only knitted once in my life and I thought it was magical. It was like looming, because from a line you get something that's two dimensional, the textile, and then the textile becomes three dimensional. I mean it's just miraculous. It seems to me a similar sense of awe about the materials you are transforming is manifested in your work. You never obliterate the miracle of the cloth. It always maintains its primacy, its identity and presence.

I sense your interest in kinds of solutions that other designers don't care about, partially because there are easier solutions.

Spring 1995 Look 68 Sketches by Yeohlee See pages 107, 108, 109

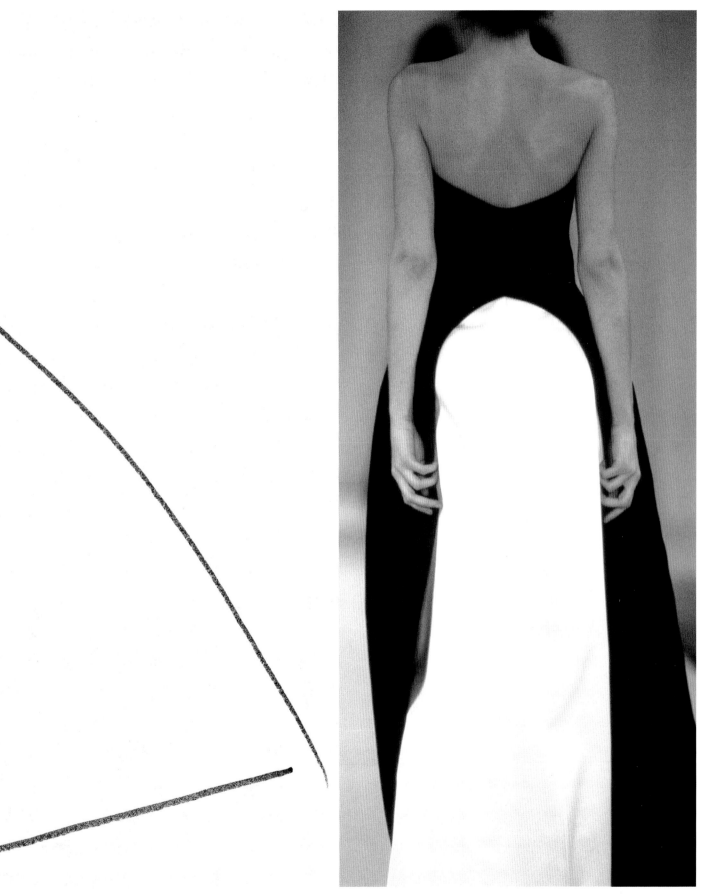

Spring 1995 Look 68 Black double faced silk satin strapless evening gown with white underskirt

photo Alan Crespo

Spring 1995 Look 68 Black double faced satin strapless evening gown with white underskirt

I understand that: to have no waste and have lots of variations in patterns. You, on the other hand, love the seam, you really do. You play with it a lot. While there's a kind of inherent reductivism in your thinking, it's not minimalist, but rather a gravitation to the most economical expression. Your impulse is always to create something that is the most concise representation of that idea, whatever that idea might be.

YEOHLEE > *There's another side to all of this, of course. It's one thing to explore all these ideas and so on, but I'm still faced with running a business as well; and while I'm developing all these ideas and playing with them, I also have to make things that are marketable. So that has some effect on the work as well.*

HK > How does that manifest itself in your work though? Is it about things, really pragmatic things, like sizing, the process of manufacturing and being able to represent a detail that you fall in love with that will probably get massacred in production?

YEOHLEE > *No, to me the part that's the most interesting is being able to make bestsellers.*

HK > But if you want to make a bestseller, couldn't you just do a really conventional ballgown?

YEOHLEE > *No. You see, it has to be intellectually satisfying, so I have to treat myself by making a bestseller out something that is a one size fits all. But then the manufacturing process*

has already buttressed the creative process, because making a one size fits all makes it extremely efficient to manufacture. Right?

Remember that when I first started, I was only one person running the whole works. So the first huge order I got I had to cut it all myself. I had a friend from school come in and he said that we should play "The Flight of the Bumble Bee" as the two of us cut 200 capes. Can you imagine? So I think my experience is rather interesting, because I had to make this process work for me on all these different levels.

HK > I think that there are a lot of people who do extraordinarily creative things that never have any kind of commercial viability. That doesn't diminish our assessment of their creativity at all. And there are other people who are tremendously successful commercially, but really sacrifice any impulse to creativity. Then there's a band in the middle who are constantly struggling with the sense that it's not only about commerce. Designers who believe that the work has to be commercially viable, but also that the whole reason for being in the system is to be able to explore their own interests – that's where potentially the most exciting work can occur.

I've worked on a lot of exhibitions where we have designs that are tremendously interesting, but remain purely in the world of the designer's mind in the end because they have no viability in terms of a public. But to have the designs on people, to have clothing fulfill its ultimate requirement, to be worn, would seem to be the ultimate aspiration. To remain creatively free and still have that as an end result.

YEOHLEE > *That's what I've always been juggling with. But I think that today I'm more comfortable with exploring more of these aspects that interest me than not because I've come to realize that there are a lot of people who understand it and are interested in it and that support it.*

HK > The thing about your work though, is that some of the problems you set up for yourself are difficult. If you were to really explore and exploit them without self-imposed constraints, I don't think you'd end up with what you design. You always have in the back of your mind that you are creating clothing. You never let the process or the exploration overwhelm the end intention. That's why, even when you've inserted points of irony or paradox in your construction of a garment, the design never removes itself from an overall impression of beauty. Your work is always elegant. There's a consistently refined fine sense of proportion and line. Those concerns are not things that you dismiss in the impulse to do something novel, to satiate your impulse to the weirdly new. Which, as we've discussed, you have.

YEOHLEE > *Well, it can be put more plainly than that. The trick is to solve inherent problems of how one has to get oneself together in an interesting manner, in a manner that's perhaps not been thought of before. But in the end it has to serve your own needs. You have to be able to get up in the morning and get dressed with a minimum of fuss, and it has to take you through many different environments and work within those environments. The biggest compliment somebody can pay me is to say," I loved your show. It looks so wearable". That indeed is a big compliment. Because how many people can go to a show and come away feeling that they saw something really beautiful, and really great and that is immensely wearable? To me, that's true success.*

FASHION: YEOHLEE TENG
RICHARD FLOOD

Entrance to the exhibition "Yeohlee Teng : Fashion" PS 1, Long Island City, New York January 22–March 18, 1984

In *The Structures of Everyday Life*, Fernand Braudel states: "The history of costume is less anecdotal than would appear. It touches on every issue – raw materials, production processes, manufacturing costs, cultural stability, fashion and social hierarchy. Subject to incessant change, costume everywhere is a persistent reminder of social position". In her catalog comments for the "Intimate Architecture" exhibition at MIT's Hayden Gallery, Yeohlee Teng states: "Clothes have magic. Their geometry forms shapes that can lend a wearer power". In both quotations, there is an awareness and acceptance of fashion's inherent hieratic structure. What is particularly interesting in Teng's remarks is the allegation of totemic function – of something beyond the measurable phenomena cited by Braudel. This is entirely appropriate insofar as Braudel is dealing in history and Teng in seduction.

If one were to search for historical antecedents to Teng's designs, one appropriate, albeit romantic source might be the Spanish court of the 16th century. Under Philip III and IV, only the elegant sobriety of impeccably tailored, inevitably black garments was acceptable. For the Spanish monarchs, black not only implied high moral purpose, it promoted a theater of rarified ritual behavior. Similarly, Teng has invested in the emblematic formality of black. So too, she plays with it as an indicator of Mandarin presence. In her more ambitious garments, there is more than just a hint of the kind of luxe fetishism that might overtake an aristocratic order of nuns cloistered in a Ken Russell movie. This is serious glamor, but it is also fun.

While Teng's garments move freely through the approved vocabulary of 20th-century geometric forms, they are equally dedicated to revealing subtle rhythmic and structural surprises of a more visceral than contemplative nature. Whether it is the incisive strategy which throws her pleating into monochromatic high relief, her ability to apply piping as a decisive ordering principle, or her sensual exploration of the passage from snakeskin to silk, Teng manages to synthesize style into a poetry about the possibility of fabric. She makes clothes which, for the most part, imply functional formality. There is no hysterical bid for attention, yet her clothes are consistently dramatic because they are so confident in the body's ability to activate them.

Teng makes clothes which recall the throwaway drama of Valentina and the streamlined hauteur of Norell. She also makes clothes which fondly, sentimentally reference the whimsical genius of Charles James. The work is firmly planted in an American design tradition. And because of that, her quotation is never fussy or obtuse. The lines are clean and contemporary; the garments are made to animate – not freeze – the wearer. What Teng's garments evoke is a magical world of self-defined achievers – costumes for dancers in a delicious piece of postmodern choreography.

Richard Flood

Reprint from the catalog for the Winter Exhibition season for Project Studios One (PS 1) January 22–March 18, 1984

Autumn/Winter 1983 Black faille wired evening gowns
Handcrafted hats by Yeohlee
See pages 116, 117, 118, 119

"Shadow play"
Papier mâché
sculpture of raven
by Shirley Irons

... costumes for dancers in a delicious piece of postmodern choreography

Autumn/Winter 1984 Black wool doeskin sportswear with leather and snakeskin insets

Autumn/Winter 1984 Black faille dresses with snakeskin insets

Autumn/Winter 1984
Left: Black faille dress white inset box pleats
Right: Black faille wrap dress with white faille piping

Autumn/Winter 1984
On wall: Flat installation of black wool doeskin two tier cape
Right: Black wool doeskin "one size fits all" cape Pattern on page 155

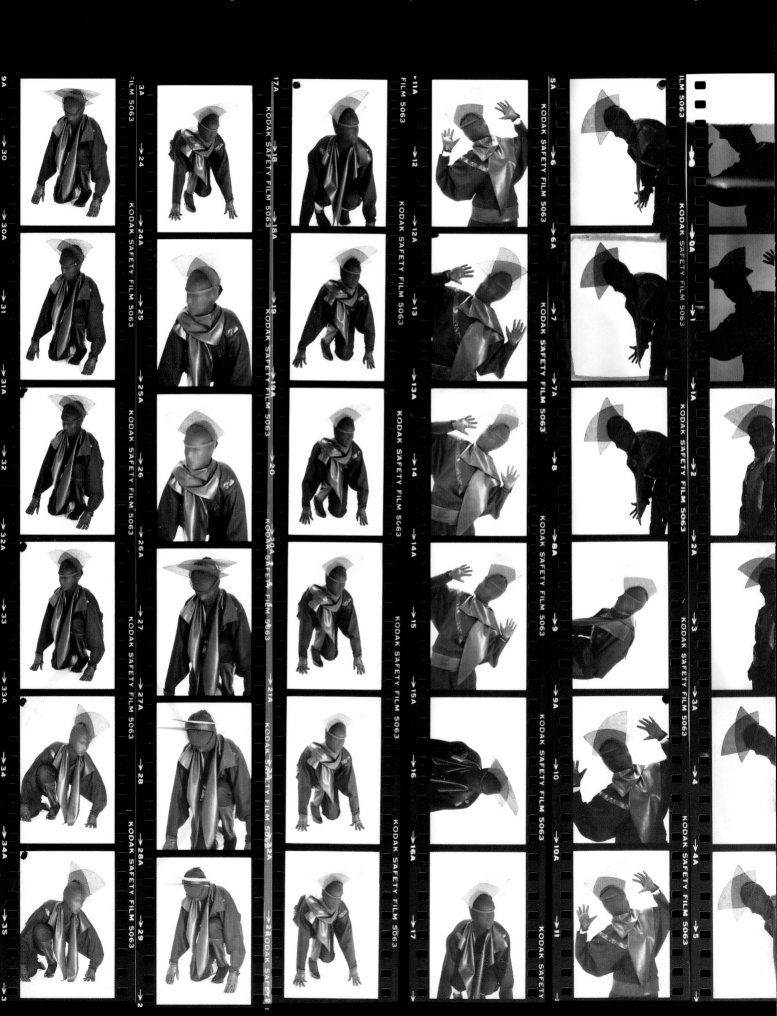

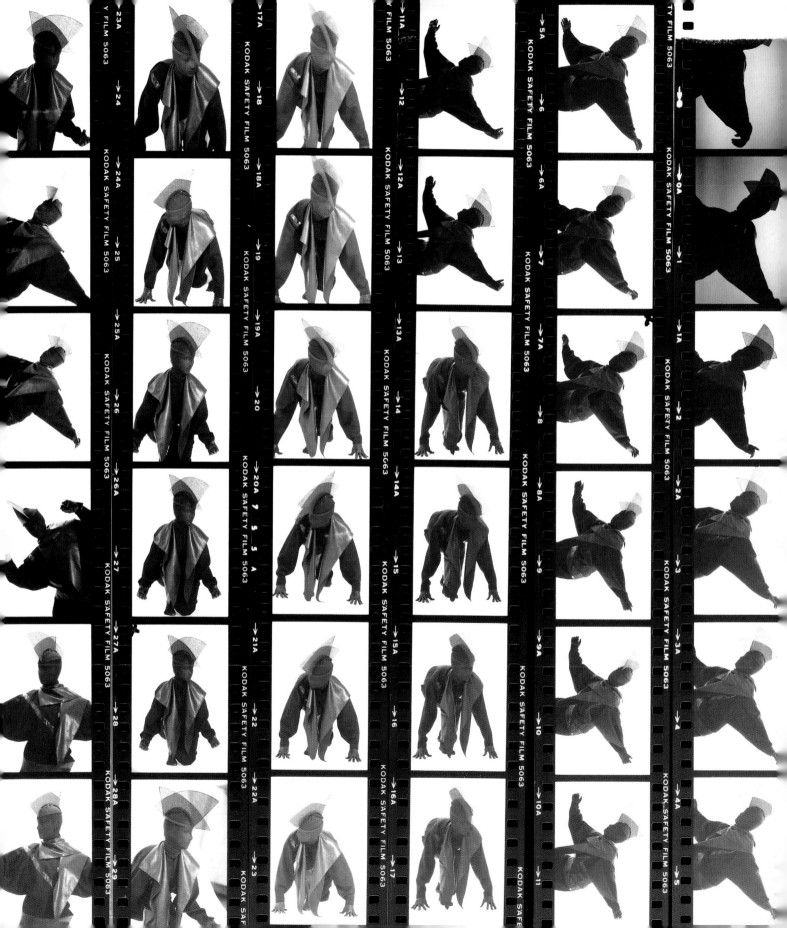

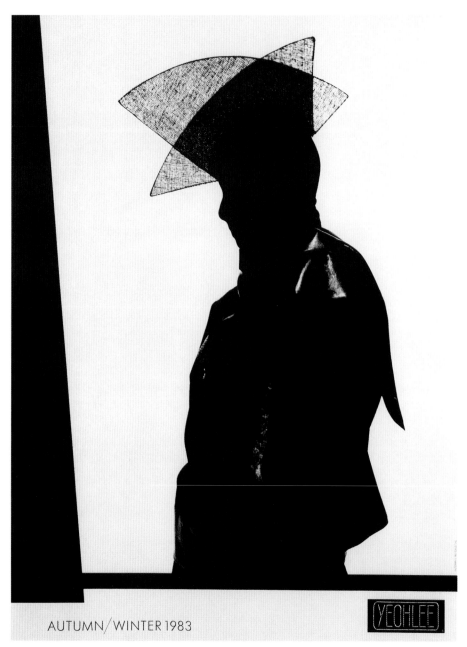

AUTUMN/WINTER 1983

Poster as invitation to Autumn/Winter 1983 runway show at the Essex House New York City

Posters Soho, New York City Spring 1983

Posters Tribeca, New York City Spring 1983

Posters Flatiron district, New York City Spring 1983

View of exhibition "Yeohlee: Supermodern Style" The Museum at FIT New York City October 22, 2001–January 5, 2002

A SUPERMODERN STYLE

VALERIE STEELE

Pattern of ombré alpaca jacket See page 53

View of exhibition Foreground ombré alpaca jacket made from pattern on page 130 See also page 53

View of exhibition See pages 45, 46, 47

Fall 1999 Look 49 "Gothic Arch Dress" in bronze/pewter silk barré Mikado lamé with reversible bronze/pewter Duchesse Mikado silk lamé See page 199

View of exhibition

View of exhibition See pages 96, 97

View of exhibition

View of exhibition

View of exhibition Pattern of cape on wall Cape on right See cover and page 8

A Supermodern Style
by Valerie Steele

Yeohlee Teng is unusual among fashion designers in that she is known for the rigorous intelligence that she brings to the art of clothing design. As the late Richard Martin remarked, "She is one of the few practitioners of her art who has fully eschewed fashion hyperbole to engage in a critical discourse about clothing in space [and] on the body". Yeohlee's work has achieved a high reputation among design professionals and has been featured in a number of museum exhibitions. Most recently, she was the subject of a solo exhibition at The Museum of the Fashion Institute of Technology in New York City, October 22, 2001–January 5, 2002. As co-curator of this exhibition, together with Ellen Shanley, I wanted to explore Yeohlee's unique approach to design, which combines tradition and technology, architectural geometry and animated movement.

Yeohlee's deceptively simple garments draw on the best elements of tradition and technology. She has a special affinity for "timeless" designs, and especially those that utilize a given length of fabric with minimal cutting. Her earliest critical and commercial success was with a cape; in 2001 she began to experiment with the sarong, a garment that originated at the dawn of human civilization. A sarong is a simple rectangle of fabric intended to be wrapped around the torso and legs. One size fits all, and a single garment can be worn in a variety of ways. It takes its shape from the body, melding body and garment into a seamless moving singularity and allowing the fabric to "speak". Vernacular garments like the sarong and cape

epitomize the best aspects of universal design – especially when they also utilize the latest developments in textile technology.

This marriage of the ancient and the supermodern is characteristic of Yeohlee's work, since, more than most designers, she is intrigued by advances in fabric technology. For example, a beautiful white cotton canvas jacket is treated with an imperceptible layer of DuPont Teflon® to repel spills and stains – see page 217, right. A luxurious matte jersey evening dress requires only machine washing. Moreover, while her designs are grounded in the principles of functionalism, she is also fascinated by the emotional dimensions of clothing.

"Clothes have magic", says Yeohlee. "Their geometry forms shapes that can lend the wearer power." This emphasis on geometry has led critics to characterize her designs as "intimate architecture". As an architect of fluid structures, she understands that the proportions of a garment, its shape and its structure influence the way we move – and the way we feel. According to Yeohlee, her clothes are not only comfortable and functional, they also enhance the wearer's feelings of power and wellbeing. In developing her designs, Yeohlee has in mind especially modern professionals, "urban nomads" as she calls them, always moving from one milieu to another. These are people who need clothing that works on a variety of practical and psychological levels. Her characteristic approach to this problem is to create deceptively simple garments made of fabrics that unite low maintenance and luxury.

Yeohlee's exhibition at the Fashion Institute of Technology builds on and complements her previous shows in Berlin and Rotterdam and at the Victoria & Albert Museum in London. Yeohlee's work has also been included in exhibitions at The Musée de la Mode de la Ville de Paris, the London College of Fashion, and the Massachusetts Institute of Technology. We spoke about her work in an interview, which is excerpted below:

VS > *Architecture and fashion are usually seen as opposites: one edifice, the other ornament, one classical, the other ephemeral, one structural, the other superficial. Yet your clothes are often described as being architectural, and they have been featured in exhibitions such as "Intimate Architecture: Contemporary Clothing Design" at the Hayden Gallery at the Massachusetts Institute of Technology and "Energetics: Clothes and Enclosures" in Berlin. What does the term "architectural fashion" mean to you?*

YEOHLEE > Both architecture and fashion encompass the body in space. They clothe or house the human body. Architecture is, of course, a more complex design discipline. Clothes have to be engineered, but the engineering that is required to put up a building is far beyond anything that clothing designers need. Clothing can be regarded as intimate architecture, because it is more intimate to the body.

VS > *Architectural fashion often implies geometrical or mathematical abstraction. How does geometry inform your work?*

YEOHLEE > I believe in the magic of numbers. Putting certain numbers together in a pattern can result in a perfectly proportioned article of clothing that works in many sizes. The classic example is the cape that was photographed by Robert Mapplethorpe – see page 25. Thousands of copies of this cape have been produced, and it has entered the vocabulary of clothing, but once upon a time I made the first one in my loft on Fifth Avenue.

VS > *How did you come to design the cape?*

YEOHLEE > The most efficient way to work is to design one size fits all, because you can just stack them all up and cut them at once. Because I was always looking for efficiency and economy, I needed to design a piece of clothing with a shape and proportion that would fit a myriad people.

VS > *The cape certainly seems to fit in with what Susan Sidlauskas, the curator of the MIT exhibition, had in mind when she wrote that architectural fashion is characterized by shape and structure, clear lines and sharp edges. In recent years, however, your work seems to me to be characterized more by a fascination with material and movement than by shape and structure, per se. If your clothes constitute intimate architecture, they remind me more of a nomad's tent than a static building. How do you utilize material?*

YEOHLEE > I use luxurious fabrics, and I feel that when you have the privilege of working with expensive, beautiful fabrics, you should do your utmost to conserve them and not be wasteful. When you can make a complete coat out of a single rectangle of fabric, it is very efficient. Of course, there are some patterns that don't fit into a rectangle, and then you have waste. It sounds a little obsessive to think that way, but I try to be neat and orderly, without losing any of the emotional content of the clothes. Another aspect of this is that I try to utilize the cloth from selvedge to selvedge. Most people cut the selvedge off, but you know I see its beauty and I retain it and I use it as part of the design of the garment. I can be very clinical about planning the design, but, ultimately, when somebody puts the coat on, they have to feel sexy and empowered. It has to do something emotional for the wearer.

VS > *You often use luxurious materials like silk jacquard and cashmere, but you have also experimented with high-tech, functional fabric such as DuPont Teflon®-coated cotton. You've made clothes out of Tactel, Lycra, and machine-washable polyester, as well as a variety of fabric mixtures combining natural and artificial fibers, such as cotton and polyurethane or wool and polyamide. Why is this part of your style, and why doesn't everyone do this?*

YEOHLEE > Well, I can't answer for other people, only for myself. In 1997 I designed a collection called the Urban Nomad, which was based on the nomadic way people live today. It seemed clear to me that we need a wardrobe that travels well. Then one day I found in Paris a very beautiful white cotton. So I asked myself: How are you going to get an Urban Nomad to wear white? It is so impractical. By chance, I heard about the Teflon process, and so I contacted the company, Dupont. I discovered that when you Teflon white cotton, you can spill red wine on it – and the wine just rolls off. It was magical.

VS > *It's funny that you should use the word "magical", because fashion is often associated with fantasy, whereas architecture tends to be associated with functionalism. Adolf Loos, for example, compared modern architecture to a man's suit, something functional and undecorated. He explicitly disavowed fashion and femininity, notoriously describing ornament as a "crime". Even within the supposedly "frivolous" world of fashion, there tends to be a distinction made between designers whose work is decorative and has a strong fantasy element versus designers whose work seems minimalist and functionalist. How do you see your work falling on this continuum between fantasy and function?*

YEOHLEE > Obviously, my work is strong in functionalism, but I think that functional clothes can also enable the wearer to dream and play out fantasies. When clothing is comfortably elegant, you don't have to wonder how you look, so you are free to think about other things. One is at ease in my clothes.

You can work in the clothes, you can run for a cab, you can dance and feast. Some of the clothes are Teflon-coated, so they are spill-proof and stain-resistant. The clothes, in other words, are very practical in a number of ways, but they show a sense of style as well.

The concepts of style and practicality are not in conflict. The first people to get upgraded on a flight are the ones who are dressed well, and not the ones in jogging suits. I have always believed than when you travel you should look well dressed and yet also achieve the comfort of the jogging suit. One of the ways to look good is to look crisp. So you have to think about your material.

VS > *It's true that when I travel, I find myself always packing your clothes, because they work so well. For example, your "Stalin" raincoat – see page 75 – is the best raincoat that I have ever had, and your "curator" jacket and skirt still look chic even after an eight-hour flight. But more than practicality, I value the way your clothes look. There is something a little bit severe about them, austere but elegant, like the uniform for a modern dandy. At the same time, I think that your clothes are much sexier than they appear at first glance. How do they enhance the body without in any obvious way exposing it?*

YEOHLEE > Clothes do not have to be blatantly sexy to be extremely sensual, because the sensuality comes from the wearer as well as the clothes. It involves more than just the exposure of body parts.

VS > *Perhaps, as Andrew Bolton has suggested, your tendency to veil the body has something to do with growing up in Malaysia as a member of the Chinese minority living in a predominently Muslim society. When did you begin being interested in fashion?*

YEOHLEE > Growing up, I was surrounded by women who were fashion conscious, especially my mother and my grandmother. I was also involved in staging school plays, so I got interested in doing the costumes. Malaysia used to be a British colony, so we did all these English plays, like "The Importance of Being Earnest". When I was nine years old, I learned how to do patterns, because I was curious about how things are constructed. Then later I came to New York and studied at Parsons.

VS > *Richard Flood has said that with your clothes, "There is no hysterical bid for attention. Yet Yeohlee's clothes are consistently dramatic, because they are so confident in the body's ability to activate them". Can you talk about the drama in your work and the relationship between body and clothes?*

YEOHLEE > I'm interested in how clothes will affect the wearer's posture, gait and gestures, whether you can lounge or pose or have an attitude in them. For example, you could have a narrow skirt with a slit, but where the slit is placed – in back, on the side, how high it is, whether it overlaps – all these will affect how you move and feel in the skirt. So I try to take all these things into consideration. The drama of clothes also has a lot to do with how much fabric is utilized. Also how it's utilized, because if you cloak somebody, they look mysterious. You just can't get away from it. The dramatic aspects of clothing engage both the wearer and the viewer.

VS > *Some people like to make a distinction between clothes (good) and fashion (artificial, bad). Can you respond to this?*

YEOHLEE > When certain people talk about fashion, they buy into the myth that only 100 people count in the world of fashion, and only what they find fashionable is fashionable. I don't believe that. I think that what is fashionable and appropriate is determined by how you feel. If you feel uncomfortable or awkward, then your self-esteem is called into question. I think that anything smart is fashionable.

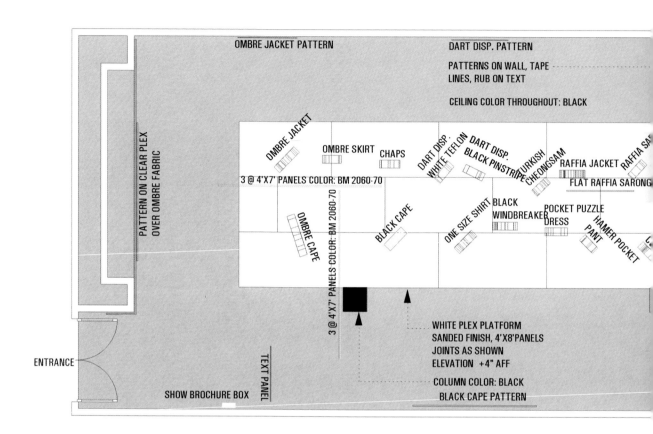

OMBRE JACKET PATTERN

DART DISP. PATTERN

PATTERNS ON WALL, TAPE
LINES, RUB ON TEXT

CEILING COLOR THROUGHOUT: BLACK

OMBRE JACKET

OMBRE SKIRT   CHAPS

DART DISP.
WHITE TEFLON   DART DISP.
BLACK PINSTRIPE   TURKISH
CHEONGSAM   RAFFIA JACKET   RAFFIA SA

FLAT RAFFIA SARONG

3 @ 4'X7' PANELS COLOR: BM 2060-70

3 @ 4'X7' PANELS COLOR: BM 2060-70

PATTERN ON CLEAR PLEX
OVER OMBRE FABRIC

OMBRE CAPE

BLACK CAPE

ONE SIZE SHIRT   BLACK
WINDBREAKER   POCKET PUZZLE
DRESS   HAMER POCKET
PANT

WHITE PLEX PLATFORM
SANDED FINISH, 4'X8'PANELS
JOINTS AS SHOWN
ELEVATION +4" AFF

COLUMN COLOR: BLACK
BLACK CAPE PATTERN

ENTRANCE

TEXT PANEL

SHOW BROCHURE BOX

0'   5'   10'   15'   20'

Floorplan, "Yeohlee: Supermodern Style", The Museum at FIT, New York, New York
Louis Muller William Murphy Architects, Joerg Schwartz Architect

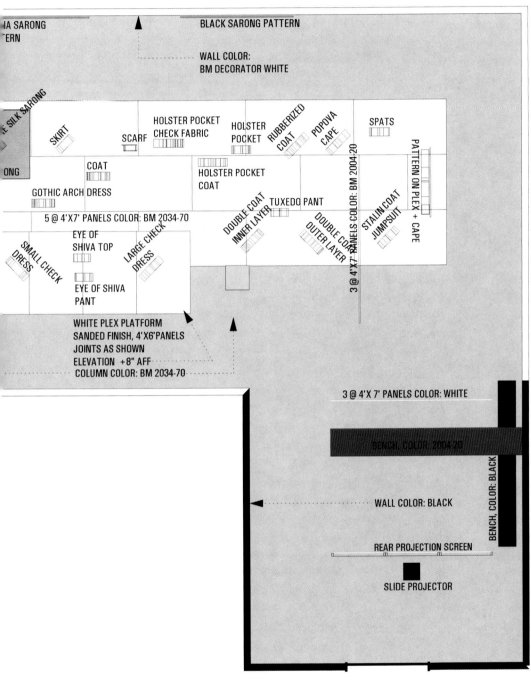

BLACK SARONG PATTERN

IA SARONG
TERN

WALL COLOR:
BM DECORATOR WHITE

E SILK SARONG

ONG

SKIRT

SCARF

HOLSTER POCKET
CHECK FABRIC

HOLSTER
POCKET

RUBBERIZED
COAT

POPOVA
CAPE

SPATS

COAT

HOLSTER POCKET
COAT

GOTHIC ARCH DRESS

DOUBLE COAT
INNER LAYER

TUXEDO PANT

DOUBLE COAT
OUTER LAYER

STALIN COAT
JUMPSUIT

PATTERN ON PLEX + CAPE

3 @ 4'X7' PANELS COLOR: BM 2004-20

5 @ 4'X7' PANELS COLOR: BM 2034-70

SMALL CHECK
DRESS

EYE OF
SHIVA TOP

LARGE CHECK
DRESS

EYE OF SHIVA
PANT

WHITE PLEX PLATFORM
SANDED FINISH, 4'X6'PANELS
JOINTS AS SHOWN
ELEVATION +8" AFF
COLUMN COLOR: BM 2034-70

3 @ 4'X 7' PANELS COLOR: WHITE

BENCH, COLOR: 2004-20

BENCH, COLOR: BLACK

WALL COLOR: BLACK

REAR PROJECTION SCREEN

SLIDE PROJECTOR

scale: 1/8"=1'

View 1

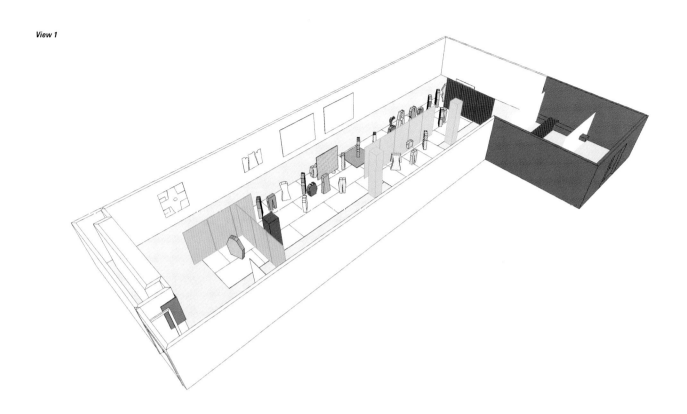

View 2

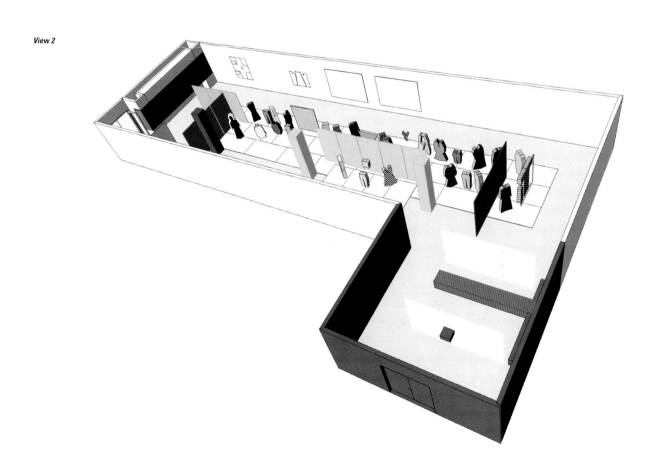

View 3

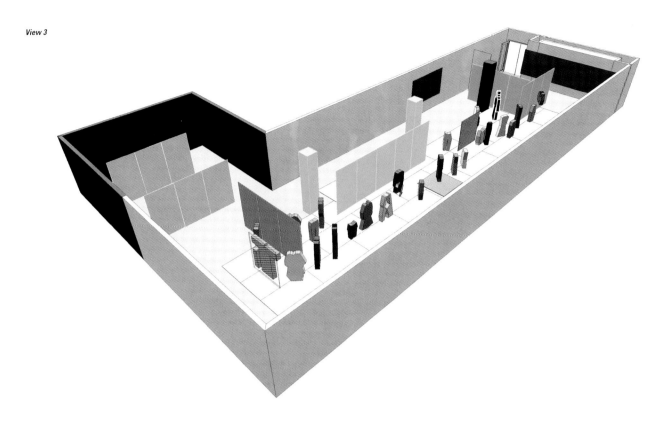

View 4

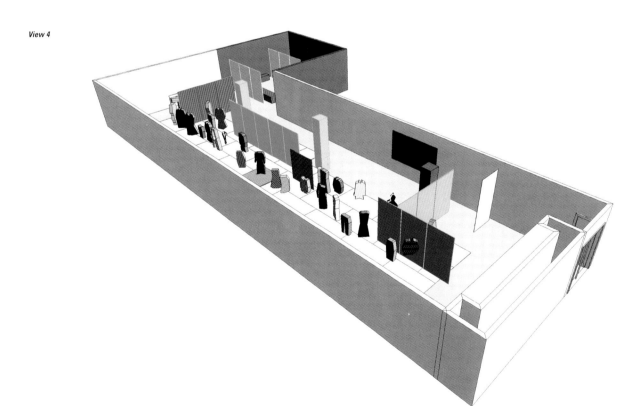

Four views, "Yeohlee: Supermodern Style", The Museum at FIT, New York, New York
Louis Muller William Murphy Architects, Joerg Schwartz Architect

YEOHLEE: ENERGY AND ECONOMY, MEASURE AND MAGIC

RICHARD MARTIN

CORTILI BERLINESI: HACKESCHEN HÖFE

Inspiration board for the exhibition "Energetics: Clothes and Enclosures" Aedes East Gallery, Berlin May 22–June 19, 1998

Aedes East

As part of the redevelopment of the Hackesche Höfe, the new gallery and cafe are situated in a new Jugendstil complex. Inside, concrete panels cover walls, floors and ceilings. In the galery this plane then provides a blank canvas for the works that are exhibited. The physical presence of concrete is not the overriding issue, or rather, afford and obviating the ideas of the structure. The level itself is not like object of the furniture and made of concrete. Through the ceiling several light boxes protrude so the only perceptions of the level.

In the cafe benches, of laminated wood and laminated are screwed walls are added to the concrete. The benches, tables and cupboards in multiple layers of flexiten windows is completed, new way of working with this material. The green glass printed with an enlarged particular image of the texture of wood is applied in front of the concrete wall.

Architect:
Ben van Berkel
Assistant:
Moreno Bücken
Van Berkel & Bos architectuurbureau, Amsterdam

Realisation:
Interstern architecture, Berlin
Redrawing: Caroline Vermeulen

kleiner Raum
small room

Deckenschienen für Glaspaneel
ceiling tracks for glasspaneel

geschlossen / closed

Eingang

100 cm

Betontresen / concrete desk

Lichtinseln / lightelements

Fenster / windows

Eingang / entrance

Energy and Economy, Measure and Magic
for the exhibition
Energetics: Clothes and Enclosures

Aedes East Gallery
Berlin, Germany
May 22–June 19, 1998

Netherlands Architecture Institute
Rotterdam, Netherlands
August 1–September 6, 1998

"Clothes", Yeohlee is fond of saying, "have magic". Yet that magic is for the designer mingled with reason and collateral with discipline and astringent practice. Not only is Yeohlee one of the most ingenious makers of clothing today, but she is one of the few practitioners of her art who has fully eschewed fashion-hyperbole to engage in a critical discourse about clothing in space, on the body, and in anthropometrics. Intellectually, Yeohlee is the new Bernard Rudofsky, offering insights into clothing as a cultural anthropology. But Rudofsky's only clothing design was scientific experiment; Yeohlee advances theory and broaches the garment not only as specimen but as beautiful, viable apparel.

The energetics of Yeohlee's work are evident in the conservation that results from her design management. She husbands every resource and wants to waste nothing. 20th-century fashion has often been extravagantly wasteful of fabric, but Yeohlee is frugal. It was said in 18th-century France and in many other cultures that the correct dress should be cut and sewn with its excess no more than the fabric scraps one can readily hold in one hand. The consequence is not a dour dress, but a design economy and a fundamental truth to the material. This is a brevity that is not merely the soul of wit, but of reason and sensibility.

As early as the 1980s, Yeohlee was crafting her designs from the single piece of cloth with its cutting, along with just enough extra material for the ties, knots, or edges needed, leaving little or no scrap on the design-room floor. Yeohlee creates a one-piece coat with less than 3 yards of fabric. In large-scale fashion, computers direct laser cutters to maximum utilization of fabric in patternmaking. For Yeohlee, that strategy is directed entirely by eye and hand, calculated on the design table.

In Yeohlee's three-dimensional art, the flat pattern is a revelation at parity with the beauty of the garment itself. (Few designers of apparel offer this paradigm: most notably, some work by Issey Miyake, and some graphic cuts by Grès.) Ironically, one can thus read a design by Yeohlee in comprehensive process: flat pattern, the scant remnants left after cutting, and the three-dimensional garment. That this process is paramount to Yeohlee demonstrates that she is a designer of clothing, not mere ornament, inasmuch as the clothing, like good architecture, has achieved its fundamental form and utility even before it is applied to the body. As it then applies to the body, it only succeeds further. For Yeohlee is emphatic about the garment: "unless it's clothing, it has failed". And clothing for Yeohlee is the pragmatic application and actual use of all that is achieved through a system of numbers, cuts, fabric selection, and design.

Even the man or woman who wears Yeohlee's clothes without knowing patternmaking recognizes the concise functionalism of Yeohlee's approach. She is thinking about clothing as a first shelter, the modular system in which one dwells even more intimately than in architecture.

Yet Yeohlee's design, if more primary than architecture, shares much with that structural art. Beyond the abstraction of form, there is also the constancy and universalism of function. Yeohlee notes that she designs for an urban environment and dresses an "urban nomad" who responds for the most part to artificially created environments that are to some degree climatically controlled, for example, the tower in Shanghai. Modules and layering, a coordinated system of dressing, function for climate control and circumstantial change, but adaptability is built into Yeohlee's sense of the harmonic wardrobe. Thus, in this exhibition, Yeohlee's layered environment is akin to clothing's strata, each contingent on another, each trapping air and body warmth or wicking away from the body in a way determined not by the single layer alone but by the entire tissue of tiers. In this, both the open space or vacuum and the structured walls or layers have related value as they do so manifestly in architecture.

While Yeohlee conforms to fashion's seasonal calendar of showings and store deliveries of merchandise, her clothing often surpasses the seasons, allowing wearers to function in the "fifth season" that interior climate-control has created for modern urban life. Too, the year-round wardrobe offers another economy from what was the turn-of-the-20th-century's apportioning of the year and closet space into four separate parts.

Further, Yeohlee seeks the maximum usage of any garment that she creates. "I hate the word 'special-occasion' ", she declares, finding that clothing has to reach its maximum utility for the wearer, not in just a rare opportunity or a structured time of day as in the manner of daywear or cocktail dresses.

She commands the sportswear principle of dressing for day and evening as being more or less the same: her clothes allow for formal expression and they answer to the needs of the everyday. Moreover, that serviceability is reinforced by Yeohlee's particular admiration for menswear functionalism.

Related to such conservation of energy is Yeohlee's one size fits all principle, in which architecture's paradigm of ceiling heights commensurate with the mean and practical for the tallest and shortest is applied to fashion.

Even men and women, architecture's inhabitants more or less at equity, receive fair treatment in Yeohlee's design. In looking not for "fashion" but for principles of apparel, she has always been keenly aware of what the genders share as needs and as human beings. In essence, Yeohlee creates eight sizes, women's petite, small, medium and large and men's small, medium, large, and extra-large, but she makes women's medium identical to men's small and women's large the same as men's medium, resulting in six actual sizes. With no compromise in pattern or in fabrication, she is able to create in the same mode for men and women.

Where, then, is the magic of design that is so spare and demanding? Can there be any room left over after Yeohlee's Thoreauvian functionalism for the supernatural or the spiritual? In fact, Yeohlee's principles themselves address the totem of clothing. In their unrelenting defiance of fashion as a fluctuating desire, they plumb to apparel as a basic human need and annex to function the other basic elements of belief. Numbers play a magical role. As Yeohlee describes it, she continues to see the numbers at play – for instance, a 9-inch opening and a 9-inch armhole – in a finished garment as if to recognize the innate structure in the pleasure of music or the forms that internally define literary endeavor. "A jacket", she says, "is made out of numbers", never adding that the designer attributes the scheme and the harmony, submerging the quantifiable therein.

Yeohlee's fabrics also attest to a spirituality that is both innate and enhanced by the designer's unclouded reverence of fabric, resisting the untoward or unnecessary cut. Yeohlee refrains from doing anything superfluous to the textile, even when she can combine the ease of a bust dart with a side seam, sublimating a conventional two cuts into an unconventional single cut. In recent collections, including Fall-Winter 1998, she loves the ombré gradations of colors that can only be used by a designer who knows restraint or else the result is pastiche. Yeohlee accords the fabric a respect, bordering on religious awe.

If fabric is spiritual – and textiles represent in countless world cultures the convergence of tangible and intangible – for Yeohlee, so too is the human consummation in three-dimensionality and in use. The wearer is no stick figure or abstraction. Rather, Yeohlee conceives of the three-dimensional person, not a diagram of front and back, but a fully three-dimensional and movemented figure. Unlike many of her fashion colleagues, Yeohlee never designs for the sole effect of the runway or camera's optic, but only for the anthropomorphic reality of clothing. As Susan Sidlauskas wrote of Yeohlee in Intimate Architecture: Contemporary Clothing Design (1982), "Despite the fastidious, economical use of fabric and facility with drapery, both of which harken back to old couture, her juxtapositions and simplicity are modern. Her geometric sheaths, on which squares or triangles float on a contrasting field of color, challenge spatial perceptions in a manner reminiscent of a Richard Serra drawing of a black plane skewed against a white page".

Ultimately, Yeohlee creates apparel closer in analog to architecture than to sculpture or painting inasmuch as her principle of functionalism is always operative. She reconciles the pragmatic reasons for clothing – covering and accommodating, including protection and comfort in motion – with the spiritual cause for art of all kinds. But it is the application and the appropriateness to needs that render and tolerate no art-for-art's sake that aligns Yeohlee with the built environment. Her clothes enclose, but they also expand our sensibility for clothing once we forsake the false notion of fashion. Her clothes give us progress even as they regress to the prime causes of clothing. Her clothes conserve and impart energy for they are the synthesis of reason and magic.

Richard Martin
Metropolitan Museum of Art
February 1998

Energetics: Clothes and Enclosures

Aedes East Gallery
Berlin, Germany
May 22–June 19, 1998

The pictures on the following pages show how the architecture of the spaces affected the design of the exhibition.

At Aedes, in a space by Van Berkel and Bos, the clothes were enclosed/veiled by the glass panels originally designed to display architectural drawings.

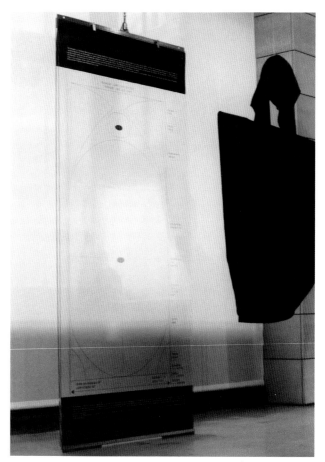

Detail of pattern See page 155

Yeohlee Teng, Aedes East Gallery, Berlin, May 1998, making a scale pattern of the cape See above

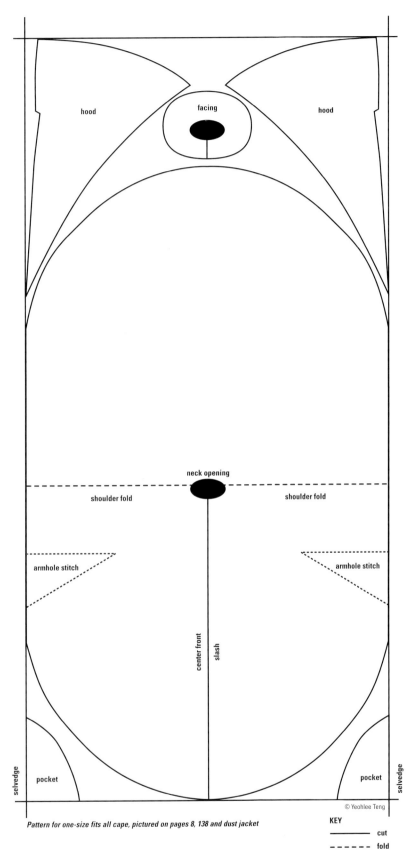

Pattern for one-size fits all cape, pictured on pages 8, 138 and dust jacket

© Yeohlee Teng

KEY

————— cut

- - - - - fold

The energetics of Yeohlee's work are evident in the conservation that results from her design management. Related to such conservation of energy is Yeohlee's one size fits all principle, in which architecture's paradigm of ceiling heights commensurate with the mean and practical for the tallest and shortest is applied to fashion.

Hans-Jurgen Commerell installing ombré alpaca fabric and graphic taped pattern on glass panels over the fabric See pages 158, 159

Two views of installation of ombré alpaca pieces with pattern in the background

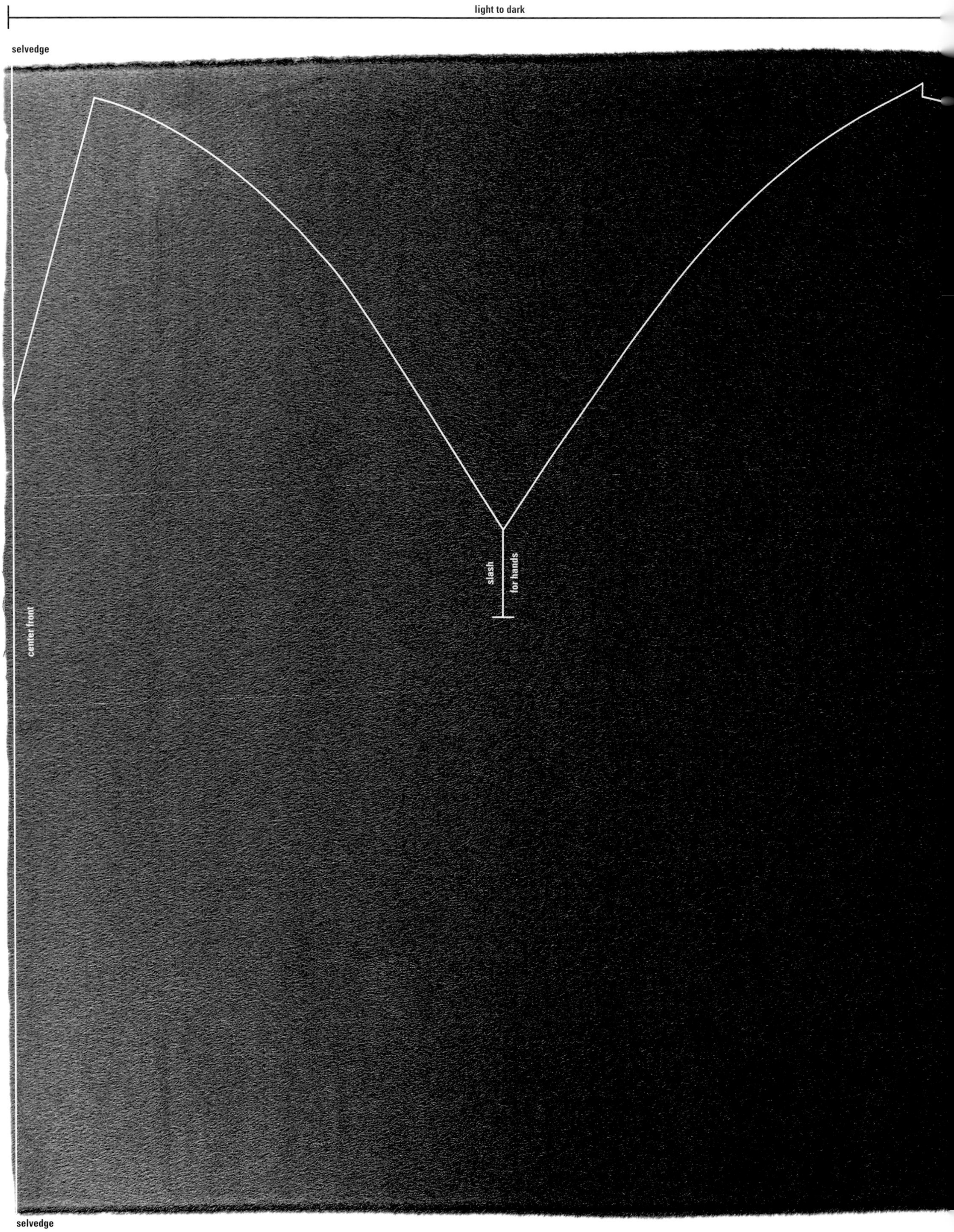

light to dark

selvedge

center front

slash
for hands

selvedge

Pattern for ombré cape pictured on page 157, 160 left. **Yeohlee's fabrics also attest to a spirituality that is both innate and enhanced by the designer's collections, including Fall/Winter 1998, she loves the ombré gradations of colors that can**

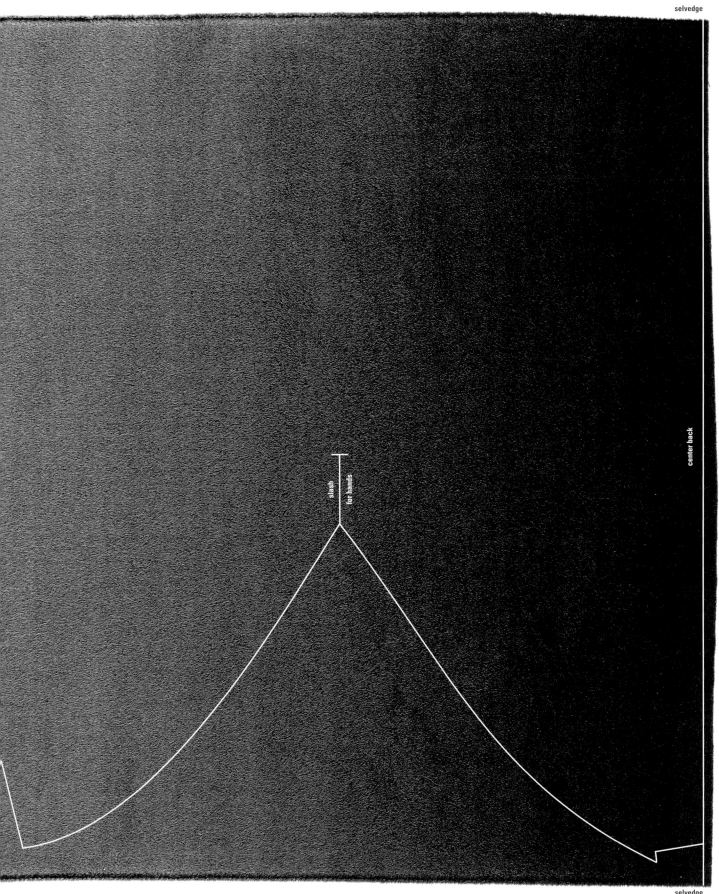

uncIouded reverence of fabric, resisiting the untoward or unnecessary cut. In recent
only be used by a designer who knows restraint or else the result is pastiche.

KEY
———— cut
– – – – – fold

Fall 1998 Look 34 Charcoal ombré alpaca cape
Black wool jersey turtleneck
Black wool/angora skirt

Fall 1998 Look 32 Charcoal polar knit top
Charcoal ombré alpaca panel skirt See page 161

Free floating charcoal ombré alpaca panel skirt, enclosed by
glass panels, at Aedes East

Still life of charcoal ombré alpaca skirt

Installation of "modular dressing" bonded nylon and wool/alpaca double coat with black wool jersey shell and charcoal wool/alpaca pants

Fall 1998 Look 1 Double coat
Black bonded nylon shell over charcoal wool/alpaca coat

Back view exposing the green stripe selvedge detail of the fabric

She is thinking about clothing as a first shelter, the modular system in which one dwells even more intimately than in architecture ... The wearer is no stick figure or abstraction. Rather, Yeohlee conceives of the three-dimensional person, not a diagram of front and back, but a fully three-dimensional and movemented figure.

Installation shots

Installation shots of the "mimbari" "one size fits all" dresses

Installation shots of "eye of shiva" pieces

Spring 1997 Look 66 White silk organza crop top
Black and white silk barré jacquard "eye of shiva" skirt

Back view

View of exhibition

Spring 1999 Black and white stripe "dart displacement" dress

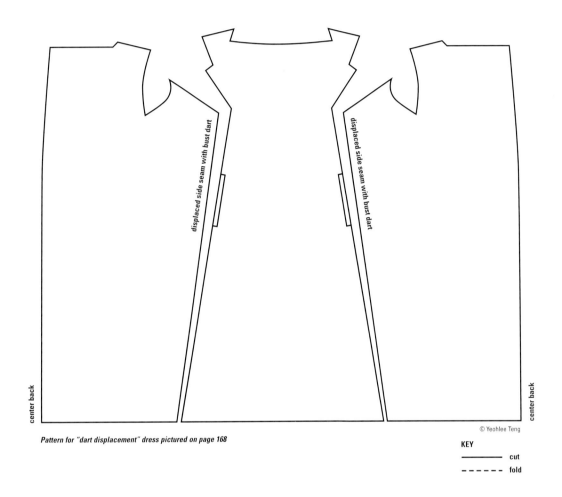

center back

displaced side seam with bust dart

displaced side seam with bust dart

center back

Pattern for "dart displacement" dress pictured on page 168

© Yeohlee Teng

KEY

———— cut

— — — — fold

Yeohlee refrains from doing anything superfluous to the textile, even when she can combine the ease of a bust dart with a side seam, subliminating a conventional two cuts into an unconventional single cut.

View of exhibition

Fall 1997 "Urban nomad"
Brown ombré stripe alpaca "one piece coat", pattern right
Gold/bronze moiré bustier
Gold charmeuse bias skirt

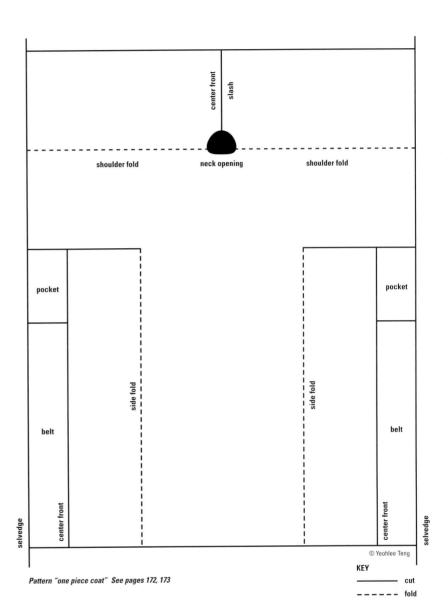

Pattern "one piece coat" See pages 172, 173

© Yeohlee Teng

KEY

—————— cut

- - - - - - fold

As early as the 1980s, Yeohlee was crafting her designs from the single piece of cloth with its cutting, along with just enough extra material for the ties, knots, or edges needed, leaving little or no scrap on the design-room floor. Yeohlee creates a one-piece coat with less than 3 yards of fabric. In large scale fashion, computers direct laser cutters to maximum utilization of fabric in patternmaking. For Yeohlee, that strategy is directed entirely by eye and hand, calculated on the design table.

Back view

Fall 1997 "Urban nomad"
Brown ombré stripe alpaca "one piece coat"

Energetics: Clothes and Enclosures

Netherlands Architecture Institute/NAI
Rotterdam, Netherlands
August 1–September 6, 1998

At the NAI, designed by architect Jo Coenen, the clothes were
exposed and full advantage was taken of the space by
installing some of the clothes over the railing so one could get
a sense of the volume of the pieces from the cafeteria below,
see page 177.

Yeohlee Teng at the NAI, September 1998

View of exhibition

Views of exhibition

View of exhibition

View of exhibition Models in foreground by T. R. Hamzah & Yeang

Views of exhibition

Fall 2000 Look 41 Black sheer silk halter tie blouse
White/black silk zibeline diamond inset skirt
On display in the 21st Century Case, Dress Gallery, Victoria & Albert Museum, London

THE GRAMMAR OF ORNAMENT

A N D R E W   B O L T O N

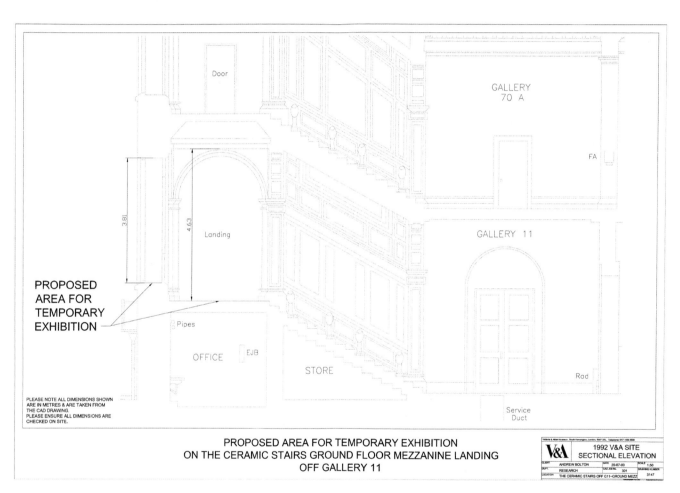

PROPOSED AREA FOR TEMPORARY EXHIBITION
ON THE CERAMIC STAIRS GROUND FLOOR MEZZANINE LANDING
OFF GALLERY 11

Architectural drawing of site

Entrance to the Ceramic Staircase, Victoria & Albert Museum, London, March 1979

Fall 2000 Look 41 Runway

Ornamental is a word that is not often used to describe Yeohlee's work. But while her clothing cannot be considered ornate by any stretch of the imagination, it is undeniably and emphatically ornamental. Moreover, Yeohlee's clothes are not simply or superficially ornamental, they are deeply and profoundly ornamental. Eschewing surface decoration, she builds ornament into the very structure of her garments. In the tradition of Madeleine Vionnet, Yeohlee views ornament as intrinsic to their construction and as acceptable only when justified by construction. For Yeohlee, its purpose is both decorative and practical. Not only does ornament lend her dresses distinction and refinement, but it often empowers the wearer and facilitates movement. The decorative and practical aspects of ornament are similarly expressed in architecture, a discipline to which Yeohlee is frequently aligned. In November of 2000, two exhibitions at the Victoria & Albert Museum (V&A) in London – one static and the other kinetic – drew parallels between the exuberant 19th-century ornamentation of the V&A and the restrained 20th/21st-century elegance of Yeohlee.

The V&A's palatial grandeur owes much to the teachings of Owen Jones, the doyen of all historians of ornament. His *Grammar of Ornament*, originally published in 1856, was instrumental in shaping the Museum's philosophy as well as internal and external decoration. It outlined 37 principles in the arrangement of form and color in architecture and in the decorative arts. Owen's 37th principle, for instance, states that "No improvement can take place in the Art of the present generation until all classes, Artists, Manufacturers, and the Public, are better educated in Art, and the existence of general principles is more fully recognized".

Today, these principles still form a useful point of departure for the study of ornament in contemporary design. In the two exhibitions at the V&A, several of Jones's principles were used to draw comparisons between the fabric of architecture and the fabric of fashion. Both the Museum's founders and Yeohlee share a passion for innovative materials and a deep concern for the relationships between ornament and structure, motion and color. By exploring these associations, the aim of the exhibitions was to arrive at a deeper understanding of the decorative and functional underpinnings of Yeohlee's use of ornament.

Detail of white silk zibeline skirt with black diamond insets photographed on the Ceramic Staircase, V&A, London

One of the most pertinent links between the V&A and Yeohlee is their didactic use of new materials and modern technology. Born out of the cultural idealism of the mid-19th century, the Victoria & Albert Museum introduced the then revolutionary concept that museums ought to operate in the public interest. Its first director, Henry Cole (1852–1873), promulgated the idea that objects within the Museum should – and could – convey educational benefit and enjoyment to the populace. Cole's vision extended to improving national design standards among manufacturers by presenting the best industrial design as exemplars of the genre. Not content to have contemporary manufacturers simply displayed and labelled, he incorporated them into the building's infrastructure. Manufacturers and artists were encouraged to experiment with new materials and techniques, and the products and decorative processes were then employed in the embellishment of the Museum. What 21st-century visitors to the Museum often perceive as an excess of ornament was looked upon with wonder by 19th-century visitors as the height of modernity.

Perhaps more than any other space in the Museum, the West Staircase, or Ceramic Staircase, as it is more commonly known, page 181, represents the concretisation of Cole's system of art education aimed at improving the relationship between art and

industry. Completed in 1871, the decoration of the Staircase was designed by Francis Wollaston Thomas Moody (1824–1886). The scheme was executed by the Minton companies of Stoke-on-Trent, England, and included a range of new and experimental techniques. The subjects of the ceilings, panels and spandrels are suitably inspiring allegories of art and industry. Although it is difficult for visitors today to appreciate the progressive spirit of the Ceramic Staircase in the same way as a 19th-century audience, it is equally difficult for them not to be affected by its technical brilliance and bravado.

Yeohlee shares Cole's vision to both promote and further the use of newly developed processes within the decorative arts. This association was explored in the static display of Yeohlee's clothes, which was appropriately situated on the landing of the Ceramic Staircase. Working in the textile rather than the ceramic tradition, Yeohlee frequently experiments with new manufacturing products and techniques to enhance the beauty

Fall 2000 Look 3 Runway Brown/bark double faced wool reversible coat
Bark/brown double faced wool reversible selvedge edged skirt
Brown/bark double faced wool reversible diamond inset scarf

Still life of scarf

Fall 2000 Look 3 Still life

Spring 2001 Look 5 Linen raffia starburst tank Linen raffia zigzag pant

Spring 2001 Look 7 Linen raffia tulip jacket

and practicality of her fabrics. She invests a great deal of energy into researching what are often referred to as "techno-fabrics", commenting, "So much of what is remarkable in fashion today has its origin in the special properties of these new fabrics". Her Spring 1996 collection included coats made from plastic, jackets from viscose and elastane and dresses from acetate polyamide and lycra stretch satin, page 189. By using technologically advanced fiber mixes, Yeohlee creates colors, textures and decorative effects quite unlike those produced by natural fabrics. In her Fall 1996 collection, a techno-stretch fabric created subtle stripes in trousers and tops for men and women.

It is Yeohlee's progressive approach to fashion that has led her to use a wide range of technologically advanced finishing techniques in her work. Largely motivated by practical considerations, Yeohlee has coated both silk and cotton with polyurethane to make them rainproof. She has similarly treated angora wool with DuPont Teflon® for spill and stain resistance. Her Fall 1999 collection included laminated wool skirts, shirts and trousers that were "air-conditioned". The coated membrane possessed elasticity, a high degree of suppleness, and water repellency with a high water vapor transmission rate that

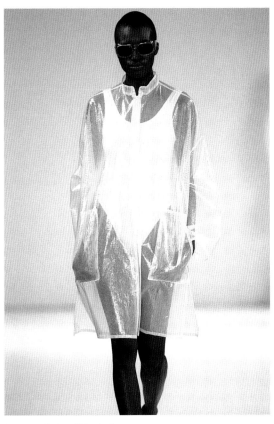

Spring 1996 Look 15 White plastic coat

Spring 1996 Look 3 White bubble cropshirt White bubble capri

Spring 1996 Look 50 Gunmetal stretch satin bodice with white silk organza skirt dress

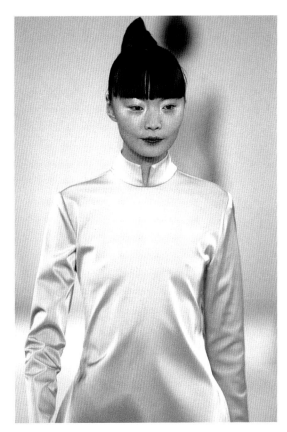

Spring 1996 Look 42 Moonbeam stretch satin cheongsam

enabled the garments to "breathe". By reversing the fabric in some of the pieces, Yeohlee also achieved a subtle decorative effect. This can be seen most clearly in a cape that used the black side of the fabric for the front and the navy side for the shoulders, hood and back, page 191. Yeohlee has also worked with Woolite, to test wash her fabrics and in her Spring 2000 collection, she introduced a lightweight wool that was machine washable. By using both technologically advanced fiber mixes and finishing techniques, Yeohlee is constantly challenging and advancing the application and perception of modern technology in clothing design among designers and clients alike.

While Yeohlee is renowned for her use of techno-fabrics, she is certainly not averse to using natural materials. Often, Yeohlee's inspiration for a collection comes from particular qualities – grain, texture, drape – intrinsic to the structure of natural fabrics. She is fond of using traditional haute couture materials such as silk organza or silk ottoman because the grain lines force light to be reflected in different directions, creating subtle decorative effects. This said, Yeohlee is never rarefied or prudish about the use of such fabrics. In fact, she defies the conventions of couture by machine sewing materials like silk charmeuse or silk duchesse satin. She challenges them further

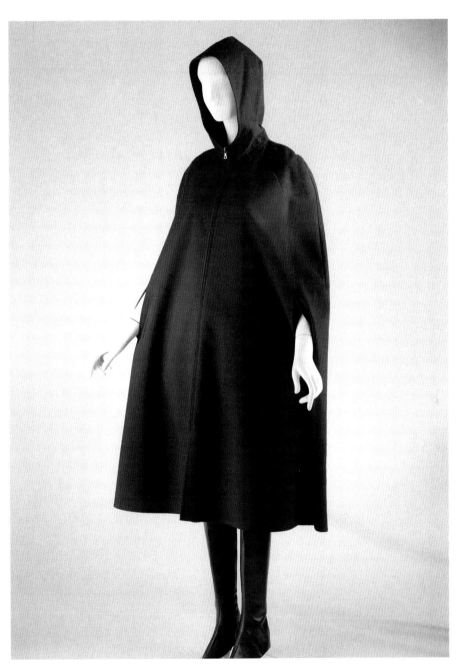

Fall 99 Look 2 Black/navy wool "popova" cape
Exhibition: "The Supermodern Wardrobe", London College of Fashion, November 2–December 6, 2000

Spring 2000 Look 14 Teak cotton canvas zip front vest Putty/gold silk jacquard panel skirt

by using couture fabrics to create sportswear. In her Spring 1995 collection she made shorts and jeans from silk and wool pique. Similarly, in her Spring 2000 collection she paired an informal canvas top with a formal silk jacquard skirt, right. By subverting the conventions of couture, Yeohlee is questioning the relevance and place of couture in the late 20th and early 21st centuries. In a way, Yeohlee's application of couture fabrics in prêt-à-porter collections can be interpreted as both a comment on the redundancy of haute couture and the superficiality of such terms.

Owen's fifth principle reads: "Construction should be decorated. Decoration should never be purposely constructed". The ornamental strategies of the V&A and Yeohlee's garments often refer directly to structural features. This is not immediately obvious in respect to the V&A where, at first glance, ornamental materials and practice do not seem to relate to the structural form and function of the building. The V&A's decoration seems to speak with a voice independent of its structure, a voice that celebrates the creative use of ornament. But, on closer inspection, it becomes clear that the fabric of the building dictates the overall pattern and composition of the designs. This is particularly evident in the Ceramic Staircase, where ornament delimits fixed architectural components within the space. The ceramic mosaic floor is not only an integral feature of the Staircase, but its pattern emerges through the physical act of laying individual tiles within a confined space.

There can be no disputing the relationship between ornament and structure in the work of Yeohlee. Ornament is invariably generated from the construction of her garments. Reminiscent of designers working in the 1920s and 30s – most notably, Madeleine Vionnet – it is the construction of Yeohlee's garments that becomes their dynamic focus. This is seen most clearly in her Fall 1999 collection where every design detail is sublimated into the construction of the pieces. Coats have holster tie pockets constructed with access from without and

Spring 2000 Look 15 Gold silk jacquard elliptical shoulder collar top
Teak cotton canvas pant

consideration in her creative process, pages 194, 195, 196 and 197. As she comments, "I look for inventive ways of making pockets, so you don't just stuff them. The right sizes and shapes matter – pockets need to be deep enough that your keys don't fall out. I'm always thinking about how to make them more useful and more beautiful".

Yeohlee's functional aestheticism, which infuses every aspect of her work, is evident in both her day and evening wear. The ornamental details of skirts and dresses from her Fall 1999 evening range have been achieved through displacing side seams and darts. By exploiting the dual nature of the material, bronze on one side and pewter on the other, Yeohlee enhances the decorative impact of the pieces by bringing graphic shapes into bolder relief, pages 199, 207, 211.

Underlying the decorative effects of Yeohlee's structural ornamentation is a characteristic pragmatism. Reminiscent of the designer Claire McCardell's mantra, "clothes should be useful", Yeohlee is often quoted as saying, "unless it's clothing, it has failed". In her work, ornament is articulated in such a manner that it enables the body to move with great ease and comfort. Within the construction of her seams, insets function in lieu of side pleats or slits for heightened maneuverability. This practical mindset also underlies her frequent use of technologically advanced stretch fabrics. But, it is not simply the facilitation of bodily movement within garments that

within, a design element partly inspired by 17th- and 18th-century pockets, which were made as separate items of clothing, suspended from a tape around the waist and worn under a hoop skirt, page 194. In other garments, pockets are formed from the construction of the seams, page 195, not unlike one of Charles James's coats in the V&A. Like James, Yeohlee shares a passion for design secrets, refinements of which the wearer alone can appreciate. Pockets hold a certain fascination for Yeohlee and are often an important

Fall 2000 Look 9 Brown/white wool cloth gamekeeper coat with holster tie pockets Cream knit sweater dress

Fall 1999 Look 18 "The Pickpocket's Puzzle" Khaki gabardine top with floating black squares Khaki gabardine skirt

Fall 1999 Look 17 Black silk shell Khaki gabardine pants with black "hammer" pockets

Fall 1999 Look 21 Khaki/black gabardine jumper/dress with square "yoke" pocket

Fall 1999 Look 13 Khaki/black gabardine "popova" cape

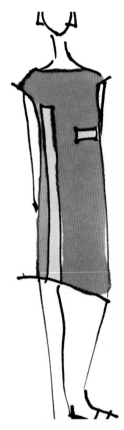

Sketch, one pocket dress

Sketch, two pocket dress

Sketch, three pocket dress
All sketches by Yeohlee

Sketch, four pocket dress

Spring 1999 Look 21 Green cotton one pocket dress

Spring 1999 Look 22 Green cotton two pocket dress

Spring 1999 Look 23 Green cotton three pocket dress

Spring 1999 Look 24 Green cotton four pocket dress

concerns Yeohlee, it is also the facilitation of the clothed body within space and society, a preoccupation that formed the basis of her Fall 1997 collection, "urban nomads". Inspired by the nomadic cultures of Mongolia and Tibet, the collection addressed the problems and possibilities of travel in a late-20th-century urban context. As she comments, "Even if you rarely fly, you travel every day. Commuting and traveling are essentially the same thing – getting from point A to point B. I'm trying to solve the overall problem". For Yeohlee, clothing must

Fall 1999 Look 44 Sketch of pewter bustier with bronze trapezial front Pewter skirt with bronze panel effect
Sketch by Yeohlee

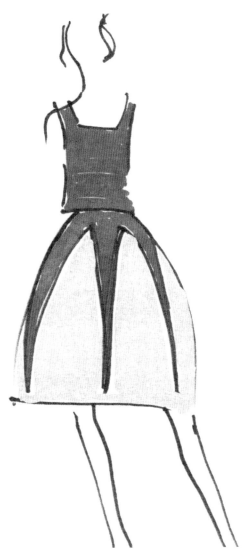

Fall 1999 Sketch of bronze top with trapezial neckline
Pewter skirt with bronze gothic arch detail
Sketch by Yeohlee

Fall 1999 Look 49 Detail For complete image of dress, see pages 133, 207

"Fashion in Motion" Flag dresses in the Leighton Corridor, V&A, London, November 15, 2000

function effectively in transitional space or what the French sociologist Marc Augé refers to as 'non-place' – subways, high-speed roads, railways, service stations and airports. To this end, Yeohlee is continually experimenting with innovative construction methods to improve mobility in and through time and space.

The theme of mobility was explored in the kinetic display of Yeohlee's work at the V&A entitled "Fashion in Motion". A selection of eight garments was worn by models who walked through the Museum's galleries. To highlight the context in which Yeohlee's clothes function, the models walked through the Museum's transitional spaces – its corridors, halls and stairwells. Two dresses, pictured left and right, in particular, were chosen because of the way in which they facilitated bodily movement through construction. From Yeohlee's Spring 1999 collection, both featured triangular insets built into the side seams for easy maneuverability. This design element was extended into rectangular side flags that flickered and fluttered when in motion, animating the dress and the movement of the body within. Indeed, the kinetic display demonstrated the extent to which Yeohlee's clothes are dependent on the body for their decorative impact. Motionless, her insets and flags fragment the body, but seen in multiple – in motion – the effect is one of dynamic synchronization. By allowing sufficient flexure of the body, disintegrated abstraction becomes transformed into integrated functionalism.

Perhaps the strongest link between the V&A and Yeohlee is the articulation and exploitation of geometric shapes and patterns for decorative and practical effect. As Owen's eighth principle states it, "All ornament should be based upon a geometrical construction". Although abstract ornament appears throughout the V&A, it is predominantly to be found in the floor tiles and mosaics of the Museum's corridors, halls and stairwells. This is particularly evident in the Ceramic Staircase where geometric shapes serve to focus and engage the gaze of the visitor. They imbue the space with presence and dramatic intent. In other words, geometry transforms a functional piece of architecture – a staircase – into a work of higher or more expressive quality.

Geometry manifests itself at every stage of Yeohlee's creative process. It is the unifying language of her work and is reflected in both the construction and ornamentation of her clothes. Again, comparisons can be drawn with designers working in the 1920s and 1930s, whose disposition to flat planes, two-dimensional forms and use of collage Richard Martin has attributed to the influence of Cubism. Yeohlee herself comments, "the inspiration and evolution of my work references Kandinsky's *Point and Line to Plane*", page 203. Yeohlee's acute sense of symmetry and proportion underlies the all pervading geometry of her work. Shawls from her Spring 2000 collection were constructed with a square and two curves. The same collection included rectangular tops and

Spring 1999 Look 49 White silk square neck dress with rectangular side flags in the Sculpture and Architecture Gallery, V&A, London, November 15, 2000

elliptical coats, while her Fall 2000 collection saw skirts in precision shaped cones, bell curves and umbrellas. But it is Yeohlee's use of geometrical pattern that is the most obvious manifestation of ornament in her work. Since at least as early as 1993, she has been exploiting a panoply of abstract shapes – dots, bars, vertical lines, crescents, triangles and rectangles – for decorative and practical effect. On the rare occasions when she uses patterned fabric, it is frequently woven with a geometric configuration.

Fall 2000 Look 40 White silk charmeuse sine wave top Black/white sine wave silk zibeline skirt in the corridor to the Fakes and Forgeries Gallery designed by F. W. Moody and made by women convicts at Woking Prison

Spring 1999 Look 9 Black cotton jersey top with broken white line Black cotton crop pant with vertical lines

Spring 1999 Look 6 Black cotton jersey tank with white horizontal bar Black cotton side pleat skirt with white pocket welt

Spring 1999 Look 5 Black cotton jersey top with white horizontal bar Black cotton bell bottom pant with white pocket welt

Collars, like pockets, hold a special fascination for Yeohlee. Fashioned into circular and elliptical shapes, her collars not only reflect the geometry of her forms but they serve to draw attention to the neck, page 204. Yeohlee considers the neck highly erotic and in her Spring 1998 collection, she examined the neckline as a "restrained erogenous zone". Tops featured rectangular and trapezoidal necklines which formed loose geometric shapes in the negative space framing the neck and face. It was a design feature that created a symbiotic relationship between clothing and the body. Yeohlee's deployment of geometric pattern also reflects this relationship. In several dresses from her Fall 2000 collection, displaced darts form diamonds that frame the breasts and the hip bones.

The shapes of one dress are brought into greater relief by reversing the fabric to contrast the matte and glossy sides, page 205, left. A similar effect was achieved in another outfit which used silk zibeline and silk charmeuse, page 205. The silk charmeuse was fashioned into sine waves, pages 202 and 205, that also framed the breasts and hips, page 205, right. In both cases, geometry is used to highlight sexually charged areas of the body. According to the psychologist Flügel, one of the primary purposive aspects of ornament is to enhance the sexual attractiveness of the wearer by drawing attention to erogenous zones of the body. The effect on both the wearer and the viewer is invariably one of pleasure. But, more importantly for the wearer, the effect is often one of empowerment.

Fall 2001 Look 41 Starburst asymetrical top

Fall 2000 Look 44 Black sheer silk dress with black silk charmeuse wave shoulder tie

Spring 1998 Look 1 Gray flannel piped square neck bias top

Spring 1998 Look 30 White silk zibeline angled neck top

Spring 1998 Look 35 White zibeline square neck tank

Fall 1998 Look 27 Charcoal wool/alpaca twill stripe oval neck oversize sweater

Fall 2000 Look 47 Brandy silk charmeuse diamond dress

Fall 2000 Look 40 White silk charmeuse sine wave top Black/white sine wave skirt

Fundamental to Yeohlee's application of geometry is its power to impose. The forms and ornamentation of her clothing have the ability to dominate the viewer by asserting the presence of the wearer. During the kinetic display of Yeohlee's work at the V&A, one visitor commented, "Her clothes are majestic – they are proud and imposing. The models seem to ooze self-confidence". Although this response was probably influenced, in part, by the height and posture of the models, it was also a reaction to the powerful affecting presence that geometry imparts to the garments. The two-dimensionality of Yeohlee's forms, often underscored by her use of stiff fabrics such as silk duchesse satin, adds to the apparent size of the body and gives the wearer an increased sense of power – a sense of extension of bodily self. This is particularly true of Yeohlee's capes, which present the viewer with an iconic, simplified form.

The perception depends psychologically upon an effect known as "confluence". As Flügel explains, "In this illusion, the mind fails to distinguish two things which under other circumstances are easily kept apart ... The extension of the total (human) figure, really due to clothes, is unconsciously attributed to the body that wears them, as being the more vital and interesting portion of the whole".

While Yeohlee's clothes are indeed magisterial, they lack pretence. Never striving, pompous or affected, they are incontestably broad-minded and democratic. Through geometry, Yeohlee's work expresses a vernacularization suggestive of traditional and regional dress. The art historian Oleg Grabar explains, "the areas and times that most consistently exhibit geometric ornament are at the periphery of major cultural

*Fall 1992 Brown/black silk duchesse satin cape with bells on points and bicolor
neck tie*

*Fall 1992 Brown/black silk duchesse bell cape with bells on points in the Sculpture
and Architecture Gallery, V&A, London*

centers or at the edges of dominating social classes … It is as
though geometry was the privilege of the illiterate, the remote,
the popularly pious, the women using (and/or making) textiles
and ceramics". In the work of Yeohlee, geometry acts as an
intermediary veil through which her clothes are perceived and
reached. It functions as an intermediary rather than a concrete
design because of its ability to evoke pleasure in viewers.

Color is rarely applied to any object indiscriminately. As Owen's
14th principle states: "Color is used to assist in the
development of form, and to distinguish objects or parts of
objects one from another". Color, in other words, should be
employed with consideration and precision.

Within the V&A, the most striking use of color is again to be
seen in the floor tiles and mosaics of the Museum's corridors,
halls and stairwells. The mosaic pavement of the Ceramic
Staircase is awash with colorful geometric shapes set against
a background of white and gray. The effect of a solid mass of
polychromatic geometric shapes is reminiscent of Mondrian's
Broadway Boogie-Woogie. Although highly decorative, color
also imbues the Ceramic Staircase with a powerful sense of
drama, a drama that both invites and encourages visitor
participation.

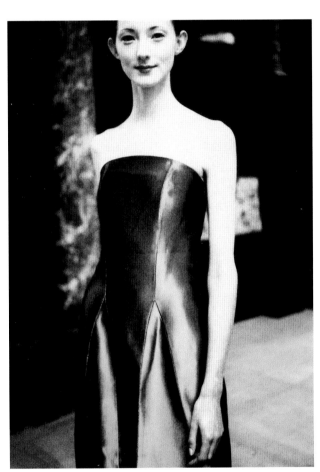

Gothic arch dress in the Sculpture and Architecture Gallery, V&A, London

"Fashion in Motion", Sculpture and Architecture Gallery, V&A, London

A common misconception about Yeohlee's work is that it lacks color. But, as she explains, "I was born in a tropical country, Malaysia, and grew up surrounded by color – buildings, clothes, food. It cannot help but creep into my clothes in one form or another". Indeed, color has been the inspiration and motivation behind a number of her collections. Yeohlee based her Spring 1997 collection, entitled *Sea, Sand, Sky and the Religions of the World*, on the habitat of her native Malaysia. Colors included aquamarine, kiwi and lime green. A similar palette was used in her Spring 1995 collection, which included the use of a black linen oilcloth with an aquamarine underside. As the fabric ages, the blue wears through resulting in a distressed, iridescent effect, pages 59, left, and 209. Yeohlee is particularly fond of mixing colors in unconventional and unexpected combinations. In her Fall 1995 collection, she paired red with brown in double faced wool separates. Keen on subverting the meanings and associations of color, the same collection also included pea coats in bright red wool.

In her recent work, Yeohlee's color palette has become increasingly more conservative, partly inspired by her interest in the physical environment of the contemporary metropolis. Colors in her Spring 2000 collection reflect the building materials of modern city skyscrapers – stone, concrete, cement and plaster. But, even within this collection, color is not entirely absent. Although not immediately obvious, it can be detected in several skirts and dresses made from two layers of the same fabric.

Reinforced by the body, particularly in motion, the layering produces subtle tonal shifts. Yeohlee also explores this effect through the use of couture fabrics as seen in her *Fashion in Motion* event. The way in which the materials caught the light animated both the garments and the bodies within. As the models' bodies gleamed through the tension of the fabric, spectators were seduced by the sensuousness of the spectacle. The garments that generated the most excitement were ones in which Yeohlee had contrasted two different colors to bring

geometric shapes into greater relief. It is a practice that Yeohlee has exploited for some time and one that accentuates the dramaturgical nature of her work.

Through color, through cut and through the imaginative extension of the body, the wearer of Yeohlee's clothing is fully present in even the most imposing surroundings. In person, Yeohlee's clothes maintained a constant dialogue with the V&A's spaces. Both are exempla of the power of good design to change the way we think about ourselves. Like the V&A, Yeohlee expands and extends the notion of functionality beyond a sterile modernism. And despite their apparent simplicity, ornament is critical to understanding the totemic nature of Yeohlee's clothes. Not only does it highlight the practical and decorative underpinnings of her garments, but it enables the wearer and the viewer to identify and fully inhabit her designs.

Spring 1995 Look 20 Black and blue linen oilcloth duster with hood
Aquamarine matte jersey tank Black matte jersey leggings

Spring 1995 Look 21 Black and blue linen oilcloth laced front poncho
Black matte jersey sleeveless turtleneck Black matte jersey leggings
For detail of poncho see page 59, left

NOTE: "Fashion in Motion" was held at the V&A on
November 15, 2000. It is an event that bridges the gap
between runway shows and static museum displays,
conveying the energy of fashion as performance;
models walk through the museum's galleries wearing
the latest designs.

"Fashion in Motion", Sculpture and Architecture Gallery, V&A, London

"Fashion in Motion", Sculpture and Architecture Gallery, V&A, London

"Fashion in Motion", descending the Ceramic Staircase

RE-VISITATIONS
SUSAN SIDLAUSKAS

Twenty years ago, when I was first mulling over the ideas that would become "Intimate Architecture", I carried everywhere with me a spiral-bound notebook stuffed full of photographs, drawings, news-clippings, illustrations torn from magazines and scraps of notes jotted down in passing. A photo of the latest NASA suit for deep space was taped next to Oskar Schlemmer's designs for the Triadic Ballet; Japanese samurai armor was set alongside a Claude Montana dress; a cast plastic bustier by Issey Miyake shared the page with a Russian constructivist dress design by Varvara Stepanova; a Sonia Delaunay theatrical design was clipped together with Ron Shamask's red spiral coat. Driven at first by intuition, I fervently hoped that this medley of images would make sense someday.

Yeohlee became one of the people I relied upon to help give form to my nascent ideas. The artist Judith Shea had first suggested we meet. Yeohlee would know what I was talking about, Judy said. And she was right. Yeohlee had great confidence in the idea for "Intimate Architecture" right from the beginning, before it was fully articulated. Her early designs – elegant, spare, fluid – offered unmistakable testimony that there were, in fact, designers thinking about clothing's relation to the body as architects conceived of a house's interdependence with its human inhabitants. Clothing, of course, adds the essential, and primal, element of the body's movement, a dynamism that Yeohlee understands and exploits so well, transforming

ingenious two-dimensional patterns (which do sometimes resemble simple architectural plans) into mobile, responsive clothing. As a house is vivified by the passage of bodies through and within it, so too does a garment become one part of a dynamic entity with the body of the wearer. With Yeohlee's designs, we are conscious not only of the interdependence of body and garment, but of the imminent possibility of transformation: a swirling skirt can be lifted to become an elegant, draped shawl, page 215; a checked coat with a simple, almost severe, silhouette is revealed to possess an interior peplum and freely swinging pockets, page 194.

Yeohlee had, and has still, a fiercely focused energy and a brisk confidence that anything can be done if approached logically and tackled head-on. When, 20 years ago, I tentatively voiced my faint hope that Robert Mapplethorpe might contribute photographs of Lisa Lyons for the "Intimate Architecture" catalog, Yeohlee immediately jumped at the idea, and helped make it happen. (Robert was courtly, gracious and generous at all points in the process – he even came to the opening of the exhibition at MIT, wearing a tuxedo jacket and jeans with a red leather bow tie.)

To be able to revisit Yeohlee's aesthetic after 20 years is a privilege. As an art historian, I have watched the vagaries of the fashion world at a distance, which makes me all the more delighted and proud that Yeohlee has prevailed, creating a

Fall 2001 Look 30 Black silk jacquard halter shirt Black and white fil coupé swirl skirt

Fall 2001 Look 30 Skirt shown draped over head and shoulders

distinct niche for herself – her clients are often architects, designers and artists – who relish her combination of austere intelligence and sensual fluidity: lush fabrics ruthlessly, almost mathematically, configured. I see that many of Yeohlee's early impulses have been sustained and reformulated over the years. She still possesses an acute desire to use fabric as economically as possible. This is not simply a question of finance, although that is never irrelevant with the fine fabrics Yeohlee invariably chooses, but rather, it is a problem she sets for herself, which compels her to discover new structural solutions. Yeohlee continues to pose and solve design puzzles for herself: how to interpret the problem of how the shoulder meets the sleeve in a way that no one has yet thought of, for instance. Or how to cut a full-length wool coat from one piece of fabric, leaving the integrity of the woven cloth largely intact. Ever analytical, Yeohlee continually presents structural quandaries elegantly resolved in a way that leaves only the solution visible to the eye.

Yeohlee's choice of fabrics has always been unusual. Her curiosity about technologically advanced fabrics has deepened and expanded over the past decades, as have innovations in the fields of textile design and manufacture. Yeohlee's originality lies not only in the variety of fabrics she chooses for her collections, but in the manner she exploits their innate properties. Often, she wrests something from a fabric that no one has thought of, or would have dared to attempt: I am thinking of the rubber-faced velvet for a graceful, fluid coat, page 217, left; the Teflon-coated cotton for a luminous white jacket, page 217, right; a washable gabardine wool for a suit that slips through the fingers like heavy silk; the conspicuous selvedges of her yak herder coats, which make me wonder why more designers don't incorporate the irregular edge of the fabric bolt into their designs. I also see an embrace of geometric pattern in Yeohlee's more recent work: grids, chevron checks, stripes, often cut on the bias and pieced together to suggest the contours of the anatomy they gently mask: a fluid, responsive exoskeleton. In one dress, a jacquard silk with a subtle color shift is pieced with facets of silk of a similar coppery tone; in movement, the body seems not just to reflect light, but to emit it.

When I first wrote about Yeohlee's clothing designs, there weren't many parallels in the contemporary world of fashion; my metaphors derived mostly from the architectural and art worlds. The former association has been borne out, in part, by Yeohlee's participation in the "Energetics" exhibition at the Aedes East Gallery in Berlin and at the Netherlands Architecture Institute in Rotterdam in 1998. In the art world, Richard Serra's minimalist drawings of a flat black square

Fall 1996 Black bonded nylon/velvet back bathrobe coat

Spring 1999 White cotton one size fits all Teflon shirt Black cotton crop pant with abbreviated vertical white stripe

floating on a white field once seemed the pictorial counterpart to the geometric severity of Yeohlee's black and white designs of the 1980s. Twenty years later, Serra seems relevant again, for different reasons. His torqued ellipses of corten steel, exhibited during the past decade, possess a related opposition of rhythmic flux and resistant tension (fortified by a monumentality, which is, of course, very different from Yeohlee's intimate architecture). Yeohlee too has incorporated the curve more fully into her designs: a wave pattern in a skirt; the curving seams of a black silk dress; the undulating edge of a double faced skirt hem; a circular skirt, which in one swooping motion, becomes a shawl, see page 215; the "gothic arch" shape incorporated into a pewter silk dress. It's as if clothing is no longer designed away from the body, armor-like; rather, geometry is tempered by modifications that admit, rather than exclude, the world, and which allow for the expressivity of the individual body. The forms of the curve, the wave and the arc act almost as narrative threads that link garments across disparate seasons and structures.

Yeohlee's idea for the "urban nomad" seems particularly apt for this era of a globalization. The veil, the burnoose, the cloak: all are elemental clothing forms that Yeohlee continues to revisit and renew. A raincoat has the amplitude and impermeability of a tent, providing a form of portable sanctuary. (And, of course, one size fits all.) Shortly after the First World War devastated Europe, Virginia Woolf speculated about the kind of society that would emerge from the rubble, which had dramatized the fragility of all manmade structures. Woolf mused that in the future people would have fewer illusions about constructing "permanent" homes. They might well choose to make portable habitats that could be folded up like a fan at a moment's notice. One can easily imagine many of Yeohlee's designs as temporary, but eminently adaptable, shelter.

"Architectural fashion" is now a subject that architectural history students write dissertations about. (I recently fielded requests for the "Intimate Architecture" catalog from Lund, Sweden and London, England.) Writers such as Leila Kinney, Mark Wigley and Mary MacLeod have brought writing about dress into parity with the commentary on modern art and architecture, and Valerie Steele's journal *Fashion Theory* has grappled admirably with the endlessly changing interface of dress and culture. Surrogates for clothing have infiltrated the contemporary art world. Artists such as Beverly Semmes and Jana Sterbak appropriate the symbolic importance and social allusions of clothing, if not their everyday functions. It is no longer quite the struggle it was two decades ago to insist that selected clothing designs could be as expressive as any advanced art form on the strains and strengths of a cultural moment.

Somehow, Yeohlee continues to fuse both timeliness – what women need and want now – with timelessness.

She continues to hone her long-time interest in elemental forms of clothing: the sarong, most recently, which she is coupling with elegant, loosely structured jackets and tops of complementary fabric. The cape, the hooded cloak, the large enfolding coat – all recur over and over in Yeohlee's work. These garments offer pragmatic solutions to a universal problem: how to be comfortable, forceful and elegant all at once. By combining the casual, adaptable sarong with a more tailored jacket, Yeohlee wants to reform completely the way women think of dress. I think she may just succeed.

Yeohlee's is a career in full throttle, so there isn't any real "summing up" to be done right now – just a location of recurring themes and structures that seem, once again, to anticipate the desires and needs of the women Yeohlee designs for. I only hope I am asked to comment someday on the passage of the next 20 years. I can't wait.

Notes on Contributors

Paola Antonelli received a Master's degree in Architecture from the Polytechnic of Milan in 1990, and was a lecturer at UCLA before joining The Museum of Modern Art in February 1994 as a Curator in the Department of Architecture and Design. Her first exhibition there, in 1995, was the acclaimed "Mutant Materials in Contemporary Design". Her other MOMA exhibitions include, most recently, "Workspheres" (2001); she has also curated architecture and design exhibitions in Italy, France and Japan. She has been a Contributing Editor for *Domus*, the Design Editor of *Abitare* and a contributor to many other publications, including the *Harvard Design Review, I.D., Paper, Metropolitan Home,* and *Nest*. She is currently working on a book about foods from all over the world as examples of outstanding design; and on an exhibition entitled "Safe".

Andrew J. D. Bolton was appointed Associate Curator of the Costume Institute of the Metropolitan Museum of Art in 2002. He studied social anthropology at the University of East Anglia and received his M.A. there under the auspices of the university's Sainsbury Research Unit for the Arts of Africa, Oceania and the Americas. From 1993 to 1999 he was Curator of Contemporary Chinese Fashion at the Victoria and Albert Museum, where his exhibitions included "Mao: From Icon to Irony" and "Fashion in China: 1910–1970". Thereafter, as Senior Research Fellow in Contemporary Fashion at the V&A and the London College of Fashion, he curated exhibitions including "Men in Skirts" and "The Supermodern Wardrobe" (featuring the work of Yeohlee), and instituted the ongoing series of monthly fashion performance events, "Fashion in Motion". His first exhbition at the Costume Institute will be "Blithe Spirit: The Windsor Set" (2002–03).

Richard Flood is the Chief Curator of the Walker Art Center, Minneapolis, MN. Exhibitions he has curated include "Zero to Infinity: Arte Povera 1962–1972", "Robert Gober: Drawing + Sculpture", "Brilliant! New Art From London" and "Sigmar Polke, Illuminations". He has served as Managing Editor of *Artforum*, curator at P.S. 1 Contemporary Art Center, Long Island City and Director, Barbara Gladstone Gallery, New York City. He is a frequent contributor to *Artforum* and *Frieze* magazines.

Harold Koda has been Curator in Charge of the Costume Institute at the Metropolitan Museum of Art since 2000. He was Associate Curator of the Costume Institute from 1993 to 1997, and previously was Curator of the Costume Collection at the Fashion Institute of Technology. Throughout his career he was closely associated with the late Richard Martin; together they co-curated more than 25 fashion exhibitions, for which they also collaborated on exhibition catalogs. Highlights of their joint work include "Christian Dior" (1996), "Orientalism" (1994), "Splash!" (1990), and "Jocks and Nerds" (1989, together with Laura Sinderbrand). Koda curated the notable exhibition "Giorgio Armani" at the Guggenheim Museum in 2000; since then his exhibitions for the Costume Institute have included "Dress Rehearsal" (2001) and "Extreme Beauty" (2001).

Marylou Luther, editor of the *International Fashion Syndicate*, writes the widely syndicated weekly fashion advice feature "Clotheslines", and is a frequent guest on *The Hollywood Fashion Machine, E! Entertainment, Fashion File* and other television programs. In addition, she is the creative director of *The Fashion Group International*, a non-profit organization for the dissemination of information on fashion, beauty and related fields. She is well known to fashion professionals and popular readers alike for her extensive coverage of the New York, London, Milan and Paris collections. Her essays have appeared in *The Rudi Gernreich Book* and *The Color of Fashion*. A former fashion editor of *The Los Angeles Times, Chicago Tribune* and *Des Moines Register*, Luther won the Council of Fashion Designers of America's coveted Lifetime Achievement Award in fashion journalism.

Richard Martin was Curator in Charge of the Costume Institute at the Metropolitan Museum of Art from 1993 until his death in 1999. Previously he held several positions at the Fashion Institute of Technology, including Professor of Art History, Dean of Graduate Studies, Executive Director of the Shirley Goodman Resource Center and Executive Director of the Educational Foundation for the Fashion Industries. He curated many exhibitions at FIT and at the Costume Institute, usually in collaboration with Harold Koda (and, earlier, with Laura

Sinderbrand). Among the most famous of his dozens of exhibitions and exhibition catalogs are "Orientalism" (1994), "Splash!" (1990), "Fashion and Surrealism" (1987), "Three Women: Madeleine Vionnet, Claire McCardell, and Rei Kawakubo" (1987) and "Jocks and Nerds" (1989). He has also published hundreds of articles and essays in a wide range of art history journals, fashion journals and popular magazines.

John S. Major is an independent scholar and Senior Lecturer at the China Institute, New York City; previously he was professor of East Asian History at Dartmouth College and Director of the China Council of The Asia Society. A writer and editor with special interests in East Asian history and in world literature, he is the author or editor of many books, including *The Land and People of China; Heaven and Earth in Early Han Thought; China Chic: East Meets West* (with Valerie Steele); *World Poetry* (with Katharine Washburn); *The New Lifetime Reading Plan* (with Clifton Fadiman); and *Caravan to America: Living Arts of the Silk Road* (with Betty Belanus).

Patricia McKenna is a graphic designer and art director currently working in New York. She holds a BFA in visual arts and graphic design from Purchase College. She has collaborated with Yeohlee for over 17 years on design projects that include print advertising, corporate identity and exhibition graphics. She recently designed the exhibition graphics for "Thermography: The Philosophy Of Heat", a collaboration between Nam Jun Paik and Dr. Mathew H.M. Lee.

Susan Sidlauskas earned her Ph.D. in the History of Art at the University of Pennsylvania, and has taught modern art history and theory there since 1984. She is the author of *Body, Place, and Self in Nineteenth-Century Painting* (2000) and is currently working on two books: *Cezanne's Significant 'Other': the Portraits of Hortense* and *Disturbing Beauty: Femininity in the Paintings of John Singer Sargent*. Previously she was a curator at MIT's Hayden Gallery, where in 1982 she organized "Intimate Architecture: Contemporary Clothing Design". The exhibition included the work of Giorgio Armani, Gianfranco Ferre, Mariuccia Mandelli (Krizia), Stephen Manniello, Issey Miyake,

Claude Montana, Ronaldus Shamask and Yeohlee, whose Black-Button Coat in White Merino Coating was featured on the cover of the catalog in a photograph by Robert Mapplethorpe.

Valerie Steele is Chief Curator and Director of the Museum at the Fashion Institute of Technology in New York City. She has curated numerous exhibitions there, including "The Corset: Fashioning the Body" (2000), "London Fashion" (2001) and "Yeohlee: Supermodern Style" (2001). She is also founding editor of *Fashion Theory: The Journal of Dress, Body and Culture*, and author of numerous books, including *Women of Fashion: Twentieth Century Designers; Fifty Years of Fashion; China Chic: East Meets West* (with John S. Major) and *Fetish: Fashion, Sex & Power*. Her most recent book, *The Corset: A Cultural History*, was listed as one of the "25 Books to Remember, 2001" by the New York Public Library, and won the Millia Davenport Award for best fashion book of the year from The Costume Society. In 2002 she received an Iris Foundation Award for Distinguished Service to the Decorative Arts.

Photo Credits

Chris Bausch
Pages 19, 21, 41, 47, 75, 77, 98, 99, 124, 128, 130, 131, 134, 135, 136, 137, 138, 150, 151, 158, 159, 161 bottom right, 163, 168 right, 172, 173, 184 bottom, 185, 186, 187, 191, 194, 215 and 217

Lia Chang
Page 12

Alan Cresto
Pages 101, 108, 109 all 1994

Dan Lecca
Pages 33, 34 left, 35 left, 36, 37, 38, 39, 43, 45, 48, 49, 50, 51, 53, 54, 55, 56, 57, 58, 59, 60, 61, 62, 63, 64, 65, 66, 67, 68, 69, 70, 71, 80, 81, 91, 93, 102, 103, 107, 160, 167, 171 left, 182, 184 top, 189, 192, 193, 195, 197, 203, 204, 205 and 209

Robert Mapplethorpe
Pages 22 and 25

Michael Morse
Page 118

Courtesy of the Trustees of the V&A photographer:
Nazarin
Pages 183, 200, 201, 202, 206, 207, 210 and 211

William Palmer
Pages 34 right, 35 right and 199

Joerg Schwartz
Pages 154, 174, 175, 176 and 177

Irving Solero
Pages 132 and 133

Yeohlee Teng
Pages 8, 26, 27, 28, 29, 114, 116, 117, 119, 120, 121, 122, 123, 125, 126, 127, 156, 157, 161, 162, 164, 165, 166, 168 left and 170

Deborah Turbeville
Page 89

Courtesy of the V&A Museum
Pages 178, 180 and 181

Karen Willis/MMA
Pages 78, 79, 82, 83, 86, 87, 96, 97 and 104

Digital Images

Joerg Schwartz
Pages 144, 145, 146 and 147

Acknowledgments

The author wishes to thank the following for the guidance, help, support, encouragement and inspiration that they provided:

Paola Antonelli

Rebecca Arnold

Chris Bausch

Andrew Bolton

Alessina Brooks

Lia Chang

Thomas Chen

Hans-Jurgen Commerell

Alan Cresto

Gabriella de Ferrari

Fred Dennis

Kristin Feiress

Richard Flood

Rod Gilbert

Paul Guilden

Agnes Gund

Eliza Hope

Dodie Kasanjian

Harold Koda

Brian Lam

Paul Latham

Dan Lecca

Irene Lo

Marylou Luther

John Major

The Estate of Robert Mapplethorpe

Richard Martin

Patricia McKenna

Patricia Mears

Matt Murphy

William Murphy

Nazarin

William Palmer

Irving Solero

Shelley Sams

Bonnie Schwartz

Joerg Schwartz

Susan Sidlauskas

Valerie Steele

Michael Stout

Deborah Turbeville

The Trustees of the V&A

Karen Willis

Kenneth Yeang

I wish to also acknowledge the wit, wisdom and talent of my collaborators.

Thank you.

The information and illustrations in this publication has been prepared and supplied by Yeohlee Teng. While all reasonable efforts have been made to ensure accuracy, the publishers do not, under any circumstances, accept responsibility for errors, omissions and representations express or implied.